Match of My Life

EUROPEAN CUP FINALS

Know The Score Books Sports Publications

MATCH OF MY LIFE

ENGLAND WORLD CUP
Louis Massarella &Leo Moynihan   ISBN 1-905449-52-6

EUROPEAN CUP FINALS
Ben Lyttleton   ISBN 1-905449-57-7

FULHAM
Michael Heatley   ISBN 1-905449-51-8

LIVERPOOL
Leo Moynihan   ISBN 1-905449-50-X

WOLVES
Simon Lowe   ISBN 1-905449-56-9

CULT HEROES

CHELSEA   Leo Moynihan   ISBN 1-905449-00-3

AUTOBIOGRAPHY

TACKLES LIKE A FERRET (England cover)
Paul Parker with Pat Symes   ISBN 1-905449-47-X

TACKLES LIKE A FERRET (Manchester United cover)
Paul Parker with Pat Symes   ISBN 1-905449-46-1

FOOTBALL FICTION

BURKSEY: The Autobiography of a Football God
Peter Morfoot   ISBN 1-905449-49-6

Forthcoming Sports Publications in 2006

MATCH OF MY LIFE

FA CUP FINALS 1953-1969   David Saffer   ISBN 1-905449-53-4

LEEDS UNITED   David Saffer   ISBN 1-905449-54-2

MANCHESTER UNITED   Sam Pilger   ISBN 1-905449-59-3

SHEFFIELD UNITED   Nick Johnson   ISBN 1-905449-62-3

STOKE CITY   Simon Lowe   ISBN 1-905449-55-0

SUNDERLAND   Rob Mason   ISBN 1-905449-60-7

SPURS   Matt Allen &Louis Massarella   ISBN 1-905449-58-5

WEST HAM   Simon Lowe   ISBN 1-905449-61-5

CULT HEROES

NEWCASTLE   Dylan Younger   ISBN 1-905449-03-8

SOUTHAMPTON   Jeremy Wilson   ISBN 1-905449-01-1

WEST BROM   Simon Wright   ISBN 1-905449-02-X

GENERAL

HARRY HARRIS WORLD CUP DIARY
Harry Harris with Pelé   ISBN 1-905449-90-9

HOLD THE BACK AND FRONT PAGE
Harry Harris   ISBN 1-905449-91-7

Match of My Life

EUROPEAN CUP FINALS

Editor: Ben Lyttleton
Series Editor: Simon Lowe
Know The Score Books Limited

www.knowthescorebooks.com

First published in the United Kingdom
by Know The Score Books Limited, 2006

Know The Score Books Limited
118 Alcester Road
Studley
Warwickshire
B80 7NT
United Kingdom

www.knowthescorebooks.com

A CIP catalogue record is available for this book from
the British Library
ISBN 1-905449-57-7

Jacket and book design by Lisa David

Jacket photography by Thomas Skovsende

Printed and bound in Great Britain
By Cromwell Press, Trowbridge, Wiltshire

Editor's Acknowledgements

I would like to thank my publisher, Simon Lowe, for his enthusiasm in taking on this project and his patience as the work progressed. I also owe Gary Double a huge debt of gratitude, as it was his forward thinking that made it possible.

This book could not have been written without Lorenzo Amuso, Sergio Krithinas, Sid Lowe, Leo Moynihan, Roy Rajber, Ulf Roosvald, Ulises Sanchez-Flor, Daan Schippers and Darren Tulett. I also want to thank the AC Milan press office, Marcus Christenson, Roberta Duman, Luke Gosset, Laura Hitchcock, Raphael Honigstein, Graham Hunter, Simon Kuper, Gerrit Lagendijk, Dave Parkinson, Sam Pilger, Andrew Smith, Mark Sullivan and Jonathan Wilson.

The chapters written by Phil Neal and Jamie Carragher have previously been published in the book *Match of My Life - Liverpool*.

I am grateful to the players who were so generous with their time and their memories. They have earned a unique place in European football history and it was an honour to collate their experiences.

Finally I'd like to thank Annie, my support and my inspiration.

Ben Lyttleton

April 2006

Front cover:
Top left Real Madrid's classic side celebrate their fifth successive trophy after beating Eintracht Frankfurt 7-3 in perhaps the greatest European Cup Final of all time, 1960
Bottom left Ole Gunnar Solskjaer has just won the European Cup for Manchester United in 1999
Bottom right Marco Van Basten grasps the first of his and Milan's two successive Cups in 1989 after the 4-0 defeat of Steaua Bucharest in which he scored twice

Rear cover:
Top left Basile Boli lifts Marseille's Cup high into the Munich sky, but not without a tinge of controversy
Top right Jamie Carragher celebrates the most remarkable turn-around in European Cup history as Liverpool win the 2005 Final
Bottom Celtic line up prior to defeating Internazionale 2-1 in 1967 to become the first British club to win the European Cup

Contents

Foreword

RONALD KOEMAN   PSV Eindhoven & Barcelona

M y first memory of the European Cup was of our whole family gathering round the television set on Wednesday nights in the early 1970s to watch these great games involving foreign sides. It was very exciting and coincided with the most successful era for Ajax, which was the side I grew up supporting. The games being on Wednesdays made it more special, for some reason.

Ajax had great players like Johan Cruyff, Johan Neeskens and Ruud Krol. I remember being eight years-old and so happy when Ajax beat Panathinaikos 2-0 at Wembley in the 1971 final, the first year of three consecutive victories. I would never have imagined that 21 years later, I would be scoring the winning goal for Barcelona in the same stadium in a European Cup final.

There was always more attention paid in Holland to the European games when they came around. Nowadays, the Champions League is so important to the big clubs because there is so much money involved, but back then, when it was the European Cup, it was extra-special. As a player it was always nice to travel abroad and to play against big sides. It felt different to the normal day-to-day world of football.

The first European Cup final I played in was in 1988, when I was at PSV Eindhoven under Guus Hiddink. It is ironic to think that we played Benfica, the team I currently coach. The final was in Stuttgart and the truth is, it was not a good game. It finished 0-0 and went to penalties. I normally took penalties for the side anyway and so was always practising my penalties and free-kicks in training. The rest of the team practised as well and it paid off: I took our first penalty and scored, and we eventually won 6-5.

It was the first time a Dutch club had reached the final, let alone won the competition, since Ajax in 1973 and we were thrilled. It was usually the sides from the big countries - Spain, Italy and England - that were winning the competition, so for PSV to win it was fantastic.

I eventually transferred to Barcelona, where there was another Dutch connection because Johan Cruyff was my coach. We reached the final in 1992 and played Sampdoria. The Barcelona team was nervous because six years earlier they had been big favourites to beat Steaua Bucharest in the final and lost. But the atmosphere in that squad was terrific and it was a fantastic feeling to win the trophy again, especially as I scored the only goal of the game from a free-kick. It's amazing to think that is still the only time Barcelona have won the trophy, though I think they are an exceptional side at the moment and it could happen for them again soon.

There is nothing better than being a footballer, but one day you have to stop. The next thing for me was to become a coach, and I joined Ajax in 2002 after two years at Vitesse Arnhem. My aim was to reach the highest level, to take a young team as far as they could go. We did that in 2003, reaching the Champions League quarter-finals where we met AC Milan. We were unlucky as it was a last-minute goal from Jon-Dahl Tomasson that knocked us out. Milan went on to win the competition.

I have enjoyed a similarly exciting ride in the Champions League in the 2005-06 season. As head coach of Benfica, no-one expected us to get through our group, but we grew in confidence after beating superclub Manchester United, a result which knocked them out. We had that belief again when we beat Liverpool, the holders, twice, in the first knockout round. It has been another exciting ride and as I write we look forward to facing the mighty Barcelona, my former club, in the quarter-finals.

One former Benfica player, Mário Coluna, says in this book that Benfica were given a curse after they won the European Cup in 1962. They have reached five finals since then and lost them all. I didn't know that and just hope it's not true! Maybe one day I can help dispel that story.

The most dramatic final I ever watched was at the Nou Camp when Manchester United scored two late goals to beat Bayern Munich 2-1. I was at the game with my son because I was Barcelona's assistant coach at the time, and I have to say it was a strange end. It was a real surprise when it happened, an incredible twist to the game.

Jesper Blomqvist talks about that game and there are other fantastic memories in this book from wonderful players with great stories to tell such as the great Francisco Gento from the legendary Real Madrid side of the 1950s and, more recently, Jamie Carragher, icon of Liverpool's stunning victory in 2005 against Milan.

As that game proved, the European Cup always manages to produce a surprise and you never know what will happen next. That's why it has been a special competition for me as a player and coach.

Enjoy the book.

Ronald Koeman
March 2006

MICHEL HIDALGO
MIDFIELDER 1954–1957

BORN 22nd March 1933, France
SIGNED 1954 from Le Havre
STADE DE REIMS CAREER 90 games, 18 goals
HONOURS 3 French League titles, 2 French Cups, 1 France cap
LEFT Transferred to Monaco, July 1957

Michel Hidalgo began his career at Le Havre. A right-sided midfielder, he stayed for three years before moving to Monaco, where he captained the side to two League titles and three French Cups to add to his honours with Stade de Reims. He learnt from Reims coach Albert Batteux and became France coach in 1976. Under Hidalgo, France won their first international tournament at Euro 84. He also coached Marseille and Congo and now works as a pundit for French TV station Canal Plus.

Real Madrid 4 v Stade de Reims 3

Wednesday 13 June 1956

Parc des Princes, Paris
Attendance 38,239

*Reims twice lead, but allow Real Madrid to come back and to win the first
ever European Cup final*

Teams

Juanito Alonso	1	René Jacquet
Angel Atienza	2	Simon Zimny
Rafael Lesmes	3	Robert Jonquet
Miguel Muñoz	4	Raoul Giraudo
Marco 'Marquitos' Alonso	5	Michel Leblond
José Maria Zárraga	6	Robert Siatka
Joseíto	7	Michel Hidalgo
José Marsal	8	Leon Glovacki
Alfredo Di Stéfano	9	Raymond Kopa
José Rial	10	René Bliard
Francisco Gento	11	Jean Templin

Di Stéfano 14, Rial 30, 79 Marquitos 67	**Scorers**	Leblond 6, Templin 10 Hidalgo 62

Referee: Ellis (England)

I could barely believe it when I saw the ball had flown into the net. It was midway through the second half of the first European Cup final, against Real Madrid. The scores were 2-2: we had been 2-0 up after ten minutes of an incredible start, and we had this real sense of euphoria. The fans in the Parc des Princes were going crazy. But that's when Alfredo Di Stéfano, Madrid's main man, started to play. He crucified us and brought the scores level.

Then our best player, Raymond Kopa, stepped up to take a free-kick for us. Everyone went up for it. The penalty area was crowded and I just jumped with everyone else. I was only 5' 7". I was surrounded by players who were taller than me, yet somehow I scored a goal with my head. It was a rare occurrence.

Real came back to win 4-3. It was terrible to lose having twice been ahead. But it was still a special occasion, and it seemed like an honourable defeat in spite of our disappointment. It was a fantastic game. Afterwards, Di Stéfano came into our dressing-room carrying that big trophy full of champagne. He wanted us all to drink from it and to share the moment. I think he was drunk with joy at having won the first European Cup, but recognised that it had been a great game and we had played our part in it. Although we were down at having lost, there was still an air of optimism in our squad. We felt that we would surely be back and that one day soon it would be our turn. Reims did get to the final two years later, only to lose to Real Madrid again. But by then I had already left the club.

The European Cup was like a revolution. This was clubs playing international matches. It was an amazingly exciting period: you have to remember that this was still in the post-war period, and times were hard. It was in the days before wall-to-wall coverage of football. There were no televisions, so when you played against a foreign side, it really was a foreign side. You came up against players you'd never seen before in your life. You had no idea who played where or how. It was an age of discovery, and that's probably why so many games had so many goals in them. You learnt about your opponents as you played them. If you were lucky, someone from the club had gone over to watch a game before you got round to playing them, but that was about it. It was exciting for the players as well as for the fans, who took to the competition straight away.

We had already seen the huge interest there was around these games with champions of other countries, because we had played in the Latin Cup before.

That was for winners from France, Spain, Italy and Portugal. Reims contested the 1953 final with AC Milan, who had Gunnar Gren, Gunnar Nordahl and Nils Liedholm - a trio nicknamed Grenoli - at the Parc des Princes, and there were people everywhere. There was huge interest to see players that the fans had only read about. It was about putting faces to names. Two years later, I was in the side that played Milan again in the Latin Cup semi-final. The game went to extra-time and in those days you kept playing until someone scored. There were no penalties. It was the golden goal, years before it got used again. It was the longest match that I ever played in. It lasted almost three hours. So we just kept playing, and waited until the 148th minute when Leon Glovacki finally got the winner. Most of us never had cramps like it. But no-one left the stadium before it was over, even though by the time game finished the Metro had stopped running and thousands of fans had to go home on foot.

The European Cup began the following season and for us players, it seemed unreal. It was an unbelievable adventure. I had never even flown before, so taking a plane to these exotic places to play football matches was just surreal. Luckily, alongside me were experienced players who'd been abroad for international matches. But this was a new world, we weren't used to travelling like people are today.

I was one of the youngest guys in the side for that 1956 season and looking back, I'm not sure that at the time I really took it all in. The older guys were the ones making sure that everything went as it should. People like Kopa were internationals whereas for me, everything was new. In those days I just listened to what the coach said and got on with my job. I was wide-eyed.

I had been born near the Belgian border in March 1933, but our family had moved near to Caen and I grew up in Normandy. My dad was a sheet metal worker in a factory. I left school at 14 and worked in a factory too. I played for the works team and that was where I got my break. One day we got through to a local final in a county competition and we played a team from Le Havre, the big local club and the oldest side in French football history. In that final, we were expecting to get whipped, but we won 6-3 and I scored five of the goals. They recruited me almost on the spot. I've got a twin bother and he was playing in the same team. When they offered me a contract to join them my dad said, "You can only take him if you take my other son too. It's both or neither." So we both signed for Le Havre and became professionals. My brother was pretty good, but a bit lazy in training.

Life suddenly changed for me and it was to change again two years later. Stade de Reims came in for me and I moved there. Sometimes fate, destiny, intervenes and that is what happened. Back then Reims had become the most successful club in France. But in the early 1950s, they lost two players in car accidents, including one of French football's great hopes, a winger called Francis Meano. So in 1954, they signed me to replace him. All of a sudden I was with the biggest team in France. It was at the time we still had to military service and just after I joined them, Kopa and I had to go to Paris where they had a special battalion for sportsmen. At the time, it seemed to me I'd hardly left the factory floor and there I was on the train to Paris with my new mate Kopa, one of the best players in the world.

When I was a lad, I did well in a football competition and won the right to be a ball-boy at the 1950 French Cup final between Reims and the Racing Club de France. Just a few years later, here I was, playing alongside some of my idols. That 1950 final changed the course of history for the club. Reims won the game, but the coach, Henri Roessler, quit that same evening. Albert Batteux was captain and he took over, aged 34. That was the beginning of the great Reims story.

Batteux transformed the club. He was an exceptional coach. I would say he was 'Coach of the Century' in France. He was an amazing man. I never heard him say anything negative about football. It was always about playing football the way it should be played. Batteux never put the result before style. He wanted us to play good football and wanted us to enjoy our football. It was all about short passes, technical ability and a collective spirit. We played fast one- or two-touch football, and he was able to align different styles of players to form a homogenous unit.

He never had a negative word for us. There was always a positive spin. He would never tell us to get stuck in, to kick somebody, or to take someone out of the game. His ethics were pure. It was all about playing football the way it should be played. They didn't call our style of play 'champagne football' for nothing. Reims is in the heart of the champagne region and we played *le jeu á la rémoise*. But they used the term 'champagne football' because of the way we approached the game. It was football as a celebration. There were bubbles in our game.

Despite the success, Reims was a simple club. It was a little club. There were only three men running it. The president, Henri Germaine, was a local champagne merchant, then Batteux, and the general secretary, who was called Perchat. The club boiled down to those three men, an office and the fans.

There was no real structure. This is why after the golden period, the club faded away. We had no training-ground. We played on a field lent to us by the owner of a local champagne company with a cinder running-track around the outside. Some of the guys trained in spikes so they could run on the track.

There was also no money to buy players, so the club was forced to use locals who came up through the system. Kopa came in from Angers and I came from Le Havre, but most of the team were local lads. Little by little, the lack of infrastructure and insufficient funds meant that the quality had to drop.

You can't always produce a high enough quality of players. But back then it was a formidable and very exciting period for us. Batteux was a self-taught man, from a family of 11 children, and he created a real family atmosphere at the club. His house was always open for us. It was like our changing-room. I was in the army at the same time as Kopa and I used to live in Paris and had to travel up for matches. I knew I could always stay with Batteux if I wanted.

He was a man who was years ahead of his time. It was as if he had invented football training. It was totally different from anything being done elsewhere and it was so good that even when I was coach of the France team 25 years later, I was using some of the things I learnt from him. Batteux had the gift of the gab. He was always able to find the right thing to say to each player, and yet he never wasted words. His team talks were a model of simplicity and efficiency. His philosophy revolved around the beauty of the game. He married beauty with winning style. I always tried to preach the same thing myself when I became a coach.

So there we were in the European Cup, and our first game was against AGF of Aarhus from Denmark. We won 4-2 on aggregate and were drawn against Vörös Lobogó of Hungary. That game was a real test. They were the Hungarian champions, because this was the real European Cup and many of their players were in the team that had thrashed England at Wembley in 1953.

They had an excellent team, and their technique was incredible, based on a passing game that was spectacular. In those days, the players were more important than the tactics and the games were very often more open. But that first game was amazing because we won 4-2. Kopa was fantastic and his dribbling skills really wound them up.

What was most troublesome for other teams was that Kopa played in a position that didn't exist in those days. Back then we had a front line of five players and although Kopa wore the No 9 shirt, he didn't play as an out-and-out striker. He was perhaps the prototype of what people call today the nine-and-a-half.

The Hungarians were employing a similar system in that their centre-forward Nandor Hidegkuti was dropping deep, but Kopa outplayed everyone that night. Kopa was the player who symbolised *le jeu á la rémoise*. It was all about short passes, and fast slick, technical skills. He was the greatest player of his time. He had tremendous vision and the ball seemed to be drawn to him as though he were a magnet. He was a small guy, but he had big powerful thighs, a low centre of gravity, fantastic balance, and a great touch. He had a wonderful ability on the ball and this great talent for holding the ball until precisely the right moment, when he would put through Glovacki, who we used to call *la fleche*, The Arrow. That's the way we scored a lot of our goals, one of which came against Vörös

Lobogó: a Kopa pass to Glovacki, who sprinted clear of the defence to score.

Kopa had great dribbling skills as well. You just couldn't get the ball off him. His game was based on his ability to accelerate over short stretches. He had a style of dribbling all of his own, based on a kind of stop-start way of running which would mesmerise defenders. Very few players could stay with him.

When we went over there for the return, we found ourselves in a nasty climate. The atmosphere was horrible. Their fans were over-excited and some of things that happened in the game would never be allowed today. In fact, I have never played in such a violent game. We led 4-1 at one stage in Budapest, playing fantastic football and again, Kopa was just extraordinary.

Kopa was also a very bright footballer. He was the organiser, Batteux's mouthpiece in the way Dider Deschamps used to be for Aimé Jacquet. Kopa knew how Batteux wanted the team to play. He was capable of adjusting the tactics during a game, and woe betide you if you didn't play the way he wanted. He was a strong-minded man.

From the start of the game, Vörös Lobogó tried to make it a physical contest. There were a lot of fouls and we got very little protection. I remember in those days when the ball went out, there were no ball-boys. One of our guys went to get the ball for their goalkeeper and when he ran back to give the ball to the guy, he got punched in the stomach. Some dreadful things happened. We were cruising, but they started turning on the pressure. They kicked Kopa off the park and it was a bit hairy when they got it back to 4-4, but we held on for a famous victory.

We beat Hibernian in the semi-finals and suddenly we were up against Real Madrid in the final. The whole of France was excited. It was the first European Cup final and because it was created thanks to initiative of French daily newspaper *L'Equipe*, the final was held in Paris. We trained as normal that week, with Batteux doing things his way. He brought in a PE teacher, which was unusual in those days, and got us working on our physique. He was so far ahead of his time. But most of the training was with the ball. There were two things he used to make us do. We played 8v8 on a full-size pitch to help us improve our long passes and the timing of long runs, and it also helped our stamina. We always finished with a 4v4 game on a basketball court. That was all about technique, precision and losing markers in a tiny perimeter.

On the night of the match, we took the bus into the stadium. There were people at the roadside waving flags and clapping excitedly. There was a tremendous buzz. And the crowd inside the Parc des Princes was fantastic, roaring us on.

Before the 1956 final, everyone knew that Kopa was going to play for Real Madrid the following season. There was lots of talk about it. Despite his fame, as a man he was very discreet. He worked in mines when he was 14 and one day when pushing a wagon, he lost half of his finger. His modesty was something he got from his upbringing in the north of France. But he never became big-headed. It was nothing like footballers of today. In those days there wasn't so much money around.

The fact Real Madrid came to get Kopa proves just how good he was. This is in the days when French players didn't go abroad. He joined their star-studded line-up, but had no trouble adapting and getting in that team, even though they played him as a right-winger.

Before our game against Real, we all knew that Di Stéfano was their main threat and after having played against him and after all my years in the game, I still say he was one of the greatest players of all time. He was a man who could do everything. But Real was not a one-man team. They had class all over the pitch. I remember the winger, 'Paco' Gento, who stayed out on the touchline for the whole game, but seemed to be able to run at 100mph. Real had an advantage back then because, thanks to the rules in Spain, they could use foreign players whereas in France we couldn't. And Di Stéfano originally wasn't Spanish. I don't remember that being an issue at the time, it was just us against them. It was the champagne football of Reims against the all-out attacking style of Real Madrid. And what a game it was!

When I think back to that goal I scored, I still don't know how I managed to get my head to it because there were some big guys in there. But they came back thanks to an own goal and ran out 4-3 winners. We felt we had wasted a good chance to win the trophy, but we were still optimistic. I think at the time we didn't quite realise the importance of the European Cup. Why would we? It was the very first one after all.

It's true that in the final, Kopa didn't play as well as he had hoped. He was a fantastic player and we were all counting on him, but it was one of those things. Not one of the players or anyone at the club ever suspected him of not giving his all in that game. There were no suspicions of that sort: there was no reason for him not to want to win it with us, because the transfer was already sealed. I think the whole transfer affair just made things more complicated for him. It was in the head more than anything else. Perhaps he was more nervous than normal.

After the 1957 season, Monaco signed Glovacki and myself, basically taking the right flank from Reims. I ended up winning the French league twice and three French Cups with Monaco. I was captain of the team and stayed there for about ten years. It was an amazing time: there I was, the factory boy, living in Monte Carlo!

But that Reims team created something very special. In 1962 a promoter came along and organised a world tour for the club, the likes of which you would never believe. It was something else. I had been gone for five years and yet Batteux asked me to accompany them on that tour and play some games. This was back in 1962, and we'd never known anything like it.

We were playing matches in Bali, Jakarta, Hong Kong and in South and Central America. It was the craziest thing we had ever seen. I remember the game in Bali against the Indonesian national team: the people were so excited, they just wanted to touch us. They were screaming. And the funny thing was, they thought we were all called 'Kopa'. So as we would pass by the crowds, they'd all shout, "Kopa, Kopa!" and pat us on the back as if we were a team of Kopas.

It was an amazing period, and I am so proud to have been a part of the first European Cup final. To think, my header might have been the goal that won the first final. But it wasn't to be. It could have made me the first Frenchman to clinch a European Cup victory.

Instead, French clubs had to wait until 1993 and for another header, by Basile Boli of Marseille, to finally be able to lift that trophy. If you had told us that back then that it would take so long, we would never have believed you.

FRANCISCO GENTO
LEFT-WINGER 1953–1971

BORN   21st October 1933, Guarnizo, Spain
SIGNED   September 1953 from Racing Santander
REAL MADRID CAREER   761 games, 253 goals
HONOURS   12 Spanish League titles, 2 Spanish Cups, 6 European Cups, 1 Intercontinental Cup, 43 Spain caps
LEFT   Retired, May 1971

Francisco 'Paco' Gento may not have won as many individual awards as team-mates Alfredo di Stéfano and Ferenc Puskás, but this legend holds the record for winning most European Cup finals (six) and appearing in more (eight) than anyone else. Gento's signature catapulted Real into their golden era. He captained the side in its iconic Ye-Ye era, so-called because four of their all-Spanish line-up posed in Beatles wigs just after they released *She Loves You (Yeah, Yeah, Yeah)*. After his retirement, Gento coached Madrid's youth teams, but is now an ambassador for the club and still welcomes new signings who are given his number eleven shirt.

Real Madrid 7 v Eintracht Frankfurt 3

Wednesday 18 May 1960

Hampden Park
Attendance 134,000

Real win their fifth consecutive trophy and set more records by triumphing in the highest scoring and most iconic final, containing two hat-tricks

Teams

Rogelio Dominguez	1	Egon Loy
Marco 'Marquitos' Alonso	2	Fridel Lutz
José Santamaria	3	Hans Walter Eigenbrodt
Enrique Pachin	4	Hermann Höfer
José Vidal	5	Hans Weilbächer
José Maria Zárraga	6	Dieter Stinka
Canario	7	Richard Kress
Luis Del Sol	8	Dieter Lindner
Alfredo Di Stéfano	9	Erwin Stein
Ferenc Puskás	10	Alfred Pfaff
Francisco Gento	11	Erich Meyer

Di Stéfano 27, 30, 75 Puskás 45, (pen) 56, 60, 71	**Scorers**	Kress 18, Stein 72, 76

Referee: Mowat (Scotland)

When the European Cup started in the 1955-56 season, no-one was sure whether or not it would take off. It was still an embryonic idea and not everyone seemed to be fully behind it. Real Madrid, though, backed it all the way. They helped to lay the foundations for a competition that ended up being the greatest club trophy in the world. At the time, when it was first founded, no-one truly expected it to end up being as prestigious as it is now.

I'm very proud of having made history with Real Madrid and the European Cup. The two go together synonymously: the competition helped make the club great and vice versa. Neither would be the same without the other. I was at Real Madrid for 18 seasons and I retired at the age of 38. I played in the European Cup for 15 successive seasons and those were the happiest 15 years of my life. And football was my life.

I started with Rayo Santander and then joined Racing Santander. I was a professional at the age of 17, which got me into a bit of trouble: you weren't allowed to be professional until you were 18. How times change! I got reported for it. Despite signing the deal, I had to wait until I turned 18 before I was allowed to play.

I was a winger and was always quick, but I wasn't just about pace. I'd like to think I could play a bit too. I wasn't at Santander for very long and when I joined Real Madrid my technique started improving immensely. But without my team-mates, I wouldn't have won anything. I made such great friends, especially Ferenc 'Pancho' Puskás. He was my room-mate when we travelled for big European games.

I remember that we used to travel to matches in a little propeller aeroplane that was miles from what planes are like now. Back then, hardly anyone flew anywhere, but we did. I think that increased the feeling that there was something special about Real Madrid playing in Europe. We didn't come straight back after games like the team does now, either. The plane wasn't quick enough. We'd have been arriving back so, so late. Instead, we used to stay after the game and fly back the following morning. That meant we had time to see a bit of the cities where we were staying. It also meant that after every game we would get together and go out for a meal with the other team. And even the referee. Most of the time it was pretty good fun and we all got on very well, but it could be pretty tense sometimes. I guess that's inevitable really. If you'd had an argument with an opponent during the game or if the tackles had been flying in, it wasn't much fun having to sit there and stare at him over dinner! But that was what we did and you couldn't get out of it. That way the matches didn't end with the final whistle. They would carry on into the night with the meal. I think what UEFA were trying to do back then was encourage a sense of fraternity and brotherhood between the teams and the players, a feeling of fair play. Sometimes it worked, and sometimes it didn't.

Anyway, it was fantastic for me to be able to spend time with Pancho. What a player! How he could strike a ball! Everyone called him *cañoncito, pum!* (meaning 'little cannon, bang!'). We were a real team and we used to have great fun together. Getting on together and having a good time was a big part of our success and people used to go to the stadium wondering how many goals we were going to score this time. They knew we would win, but they'd be there gambling on how many we would win by. Quite a lot of money passed hands. We always felt confident, but we weren't quite as cocky as the fans were!

Because we won six European Cups and got to eight finals, people seem to think that we walked it. We didn't. It's important to make clear that it wasn't easy. In terms of consistency we were the best team in Europe - I think our record shows that - but we had to really fight for what we achieved and it certainly wasn't a pushover. We came up against some great sides, like AC Milan, Stade de Reims, who were superb even though they have become forgotten since, Benfica, even our old rivals Barcelona and Atlético Madrid.

We beat Barcelona in the semi-finals of the 1960 campaign, the year we were bidding for a fifth straight title. Of course Barca were our deadly rivals in Spain and they actually pipped us to the League title on goal average that season, partly as revenge for us defeating them 6-2 on aggregate to knock them out of the European Cup. I remember their fairly eccentric Argentine manager Helenio Herrera was sacked immediatley after we had beaten them. He had some interesting motivational techniques. He used to gather the Barcelona players together before the game and place their hands on a football in the middle of the group and chant out loud, "The European Cup. We shall have it!"

Now we were in the final against Eintracht Frankfurt and it was at Hampden Park in Glasgow. Our coach was Miguel Muñoz; he was an institution at the club. He had won the European Cup as a player and then as a coach. He was very smart psychologically and we all got on very well with him. I would say that for the trophies he has won, he should be considered the best coach this club has ever had. His knowledge was excellent and he was able to win the tournament with the old guard and then with younger, more inexperienced players like José Martínez, known as 'Pirri' or Amancio Amaro.

Despite winning four finals in a row, we went behind in this game to an early goal from Frankfurt, who had thrashed Glasgow Rangers 12-4 on aggregate in their semi-final. And the Germans hit the bar as well. But then Di Stéfano started playing, dominating midfield. He scored two goals before half-time to get us back into it. This meant he'd scored in all of the first five European Cup Finals; an incredible record. It was a great final to play in and we ended up winning 7-3. It has become so famous for all the goals and the fact that lots of people said, and continue to say, that it was the greatest final ever. Three for Di Stéfano and four for the 34-year-old Puskás. When you look back on it, it's incredible really. We were aware on the day that this was something special. As we paraded around the pitch the crowd rose to us, and remember in those days there would have been very few travelling supporters. Most of the spectators were local Scots who appreciated the wonderful football match the two teams had served up. It was a very special occasion. And we added to it some weeks later when we defeated Penarol of Uruguay 5-1 on aggregate to win the inaugral World Club Championship.

I don't have the slightest doubt at all that the greatest player of all time was Di Stéfano. He was everything. He played everywhere and there was nothing he couldn't do. He would play at the back, in midfield and up front and he loved to win. Oh, how he loved to win! He would go absolutely mad at us if we got things wrong or if people weren't trying and he gave everything for the club. He was supremely talented, but completely dedicated too. He was a born winner, who made it almost impossible to lose. He wouldn't let you relax for a minute and you knew that he could produce something amazing at any moment. He was a true leader. He was a beast as a player, and sometimes as a man too, because he certainly had his little foibles and he had quite a temper on him. He was such an amazing player. No sooner had he arrived than Madrid became the best team around. The only pity is that he didn't join Real Madrid until he was already 27; had he arrived earlier, there is no doubt that the club would have won even more.

Looking back on it now, I feel tremendously proud to have won the tournament six times, but it seemed more normal then. We played in eight finals in just ten years and that's unthinkable nowadays. I think that gives some idea of the level of dominance from Real Madrid and explains the reason why Real Madrid became so well-known and well-respected all over the world. There simply wasn't any other club with a record that was even nearly as good as ours.

The only side that could challenge us is the great AC Milan team of the late 1980s with Van Basten. They were the reason that Real Madrid's brilliant *Quinta del Buitre* side - which contained Emilio Butragueño, Michel, Manuel Sanchís, Rafael Gordillo, Martín Vázquez and Hugo Sánchez - didn't win anything in the 1980s and they became a bit like we were for a while. No-one could stop them:

of ten games they'd win eleven. I think the best two teams in history are the Real Madrid side I played in and Arrigo Sacchi's Milan, but I reckon we were better because we went on for longer and won more. We pleased everyone, too: those who demand results and those who demand great football. And, believe me, that's not easy.

I have really fond memories of other European Cup finals we played, and the first and the third are the other ones that stand out for me personally.

The first time you win a competition is always very special. We beat Stade de Reims 4-3 in Paris and we were 2-0 down inside ten minutes, so the comeback was incredible. Di Stéfano, Rial and Marquitos got the goals, with the fourth scored quite late on by Rial from my cross. I remember that they had Raymond Kopa playing for them, who would later join us, and we just couldn't stop him, especially early on. But we fought our way back. One of the things that often gets overlooked is that our team had a hell of a lot of character as well as talent.

For me, the third final that we won, against AC Milan in Brussels in May 1958, was also very special. I would say that was my best performance in a final. I really felt like I had the beating of their full-back on the left wing and I was lucky enough to score the winner in extra-time to make it 3-2. I'd hit the post before, but this time when I cut inside I just belted it, hoped for the best, and it flew in. The feeling was incredible.

I wasn't really a great goalscorer. That was never my job and it wasn't my dream either. I would get maybe ten or 12 a season, but I didn't need to worry about scoring with the players I had on my team. If I saw a chance I would shoot; if not, there was always someone to give the ball to. I enjoyed providing goals for others more, I liked standing back and watching them sticking the ball in the net, but I was lucky enough to score in two European Cup finals; that one in 1958, which turned out to be the winner, and also the year before when we beat Fiorentina 2-0 in the Bernabéu.

I remember the third final fondly. I felt such immense happiness because when I scored we were well into extra-time and it looked like we were on our way to penalties. Everyone was so delighted and, quite frankly, really relieved. We had won two European Cups already and that one made the hat-trick. Just because we had won it twice before didn't make it any easier, in fact I think the pressure was greater and we were very nervous before the final.

You never ever expected to win - we certainly didn't expect to win five European Cups in a row - and that tension never goes away no matter how much you believe in yourself. We believed in ourselves, in our ability and the way we played, but we were quite edgy. The moment the ball went in was very special. It always seems a bit ridiculous to talk about failures given what we achieved, but losing the finals to Benfica in 1962 and Inter in 1964 was a real pity. I was captain in both finals and defeat hurt. Maybe by then we were getting a little bit old. We were 2-0 up and 3-2 up in the final against Benfica with Puskás scoring a hat-trick, but we ended up losing 5-3 to a great side led by Eusébio, who scored twice that night in Amsterdam.

Two years later, we lost 3-1 to Inter, who had the Spaniard Luis Suarez playing for them. We had a lot of the ball, but just couldn't get into the game against them. They were a tactically astute team. Fortunately a new wave of players came through and we came back and won the tournament once more in 1966 against Partizan Belgrade - that was my sixth winner's medal. I'm very proud of that team: eleven Spaniards had won the European Cup.

I think that was the first time a team with no foreigners won the trophy. I was the granddad of the team by then. They were all young lads and they would ask for my advice, just as I had done when I first arrived all those years earlier. I'd arrived at Madrid having only played ten professional games, so I really needed help. Rial, in particular, really supported me and we ended up being close friends.

Looking back on it, I realise that what we achieved was historic, but at the time the European Cup wasn't what it is now. Hardly anyone watched it. It didn't have the impact that it has now. There were few televisions, hardly any journalists and not many fans travelled with their teams. At most, you might have 12 or 15 fans travelling with the team. That was enough. You didn't expect any more. But we helped make the competition great and I think we became a great club thanks mainly to our president, Don Santiago Bernabéu.

He was the one that marked a generation and always signed the very best players available: Di Stéfano, Rial, Santamaría. I could go on and on. In 18 years I won six European Cups and 12 league titles. There wasn't a single season in which I finished empty-handed. I don't think there is any club in history that can boast a record like that.

As I say, Bernabéu was a huge part of our success, the architect of it all. He would come and see the team, meet up with us before every match and tell us that we had to be united, that we had to fight together for victory. We had to be like brothers and go out onto the pitch and do it for the club. He would be there willing us to win.

Bernabéu was like a father to us. He was stern and demanded discipline, but he wouldn't let anyone mess us around or hurt us. He was very protective of us all. He was more than capable of shouting at us but most of the time he was affectionate.

When we won the European Cups and travelled back to Madrid the receptions were always amazing. Everybody would be out in the street cheering us and partying. They would provide us with open-topped cars that picked us up on the runway at Barajas and we'd drive round the city with the Cup, so that people could welcome us back and get a glimpse of the trophy.

We would then go down to the fountain and statue at Plaza de Cibeles, a tradition that has carried on to this day. We would also arrange a celebration in the stadium so that all the fans could come and join in, and feel part of it. And, of course, we would take the trophy to the Town Hall and offer it to the mayor of Madrid. We'd go out onto the balcony with him and thousands upon thousands of people would be lining the streets below, or standing out on the balconies of their houses to celebrate with us. Those were really special times.

I have won more European Cups than anyone else and of course I am extremely proud of that. It's nice to know that I form a tiny bit of Real Madrid's history, and of the history of the European Cup.

MARIO COLUNA
MIDFIELDER 1954–1970

BORN   6th August 1935, Inhaca, Mozambique
SIGNED   1954 from Desportivo de Lourenco Marques
BENFICA CAREER   525 games, 127 goals
HONOURS   10 Portuguese Championships, 7 Portuguese Cups,
2 European Cups, 57 Portugal caps
LEFT   Transferred to Lyon, May 1970

Mário Coluna set the trail followed by his eventual Benfica team-mate Eusébio as a Mozambique-born player who represented the Portugal national team. Coluna was an attacking midfielder whom Benfica coach Bela Guttmann called "my most important player". He captained Benfica to the European Cup in 1962 and played in the three finals Benfica went on to lose in the 1960s. He was also captain of Portugal when they finished third in the 1966 World Cup. After Mozambique became independent in 1975, Coluna served as the country's Minister of Sport and is now president of the Mozambique FA.

Benfica 3 v Barcelona 2

Wednesday 31 May 1961

Wankdorf Stadium, Berne
Attendance 33,000

Benfica end Real Madrid's run of five straight titles and become the first non-Spanish side to win the European Cup

Teams

Alberto da Costa Pereira	1	Toni Ramallets
Mario Joao	2	Alfonso Foncho
Germano de Figueiredo	3	Enric Gensana
Angelo Gaspar Martins	4	Sigfrid Gracia
José Antonio Neto	5	Martí Vergés
Fernando Cruz	6	Jesús Garay
José Augusto Almeida	7	Ladislao Kubala
Joaquim Santana	8	Sándor Kocsis
José Aguas	9	Evaristo Macedo
Mário Coluna	10	Luis Suarez
Domiciano Cavem	11	Zoltán Czibor

Aguas 30, Ramallets (og) 32 Coluna 55	**Scorers**	Kocsis 5, Czibor 75

Referee: Dienst (Switzerland)

"Football is a simple game," I thought to myself when Sándor Kocsis put Barcelona ahead in the fifth minute of our first ever European Cup final. Before we got to the final, we had never thought that we could win the European Cup. After all, we had to play against the champions of all the other countries and we knew that it would not be easy. Before our campaign started, I didn't ever think that we would be champions. That prospect never entered my head.

But out there on the pitch, having got as far as the final, none of us panicked. For most people, Benfica were not the favourites. It was Barcelona, remember, who had knocked out Real Madrid, the winners of the previous five editions of the competition. But all I was thinking about was that we had to score more goals than them. It was very simple.

So when we went behind early on, I didn't think that we were going to lose or that it would be impossible for us to win. I just knew that we had to score a goal to tie the game, and get another if we wanted to win the game and lift the trophy. I knew that there was no logic to this crazy game.

Sometimes the best team does not always win, it's only the team that scores the most goals. And that is precisely what happened in Switzerland on that amazing night in May. We may not have been the best team, but we scored the most goals.

It had been a tough route to the final. The games took place over 40 years ago so I can't remember them all, but the semi-final against Rapid Vienna was a really tough one. In the second leg, in Austria, the home fans reacted violently to their team's impending elimination. We drew with them 1-1, but won 4-1 on aggregate. The second leg was abandoned after the English referee turned down a Rapid penalty appeal, leading to a pitch invasion late in the game. We didn't actually see any real trouble, but the police came and told us not to leave our dressing-room. We had to stay there for over half an hour. We took our showers quietly and calmly, and waited there for long time. When the police finally told us that it was OK to leave the stadium, they made sure we had an escort back to the hotel. UEFA ruled that the result stood and we were in the final.

We were definitely a bit nervous, anxious, before the final. It was no surprise really, because we were up against Barcelona, one of the best teams in the world. And, of course, it was a European Cup final!

We had travelled to Berne about four days before the game. Our coach,

Bela Guttmann, wanted us to have the same preparations as for any other game. So before this European Cup final, he gave the same instructions that he always did. He saw every game the same way and his desire to win was always the same. This was one of the most important games of our lives, yet Guttmann repeated the same things to the players that he always did: that Barcelona were just a team like any other, that we shouldn't feel inferior to them.

"Let's go out on that pitch, and fight, fight, fight." These were always his last words before every game, no matter if it was the European Cup final or a Portuguese Cup match against a lower-league side.

Guttmann had signed his first contract with Benfica in 1960. But when he was putting pen to paper on the deal, he had asked the board for a bonus, the equivalent of 1,000 euros, if he led the team to success in the European Cup. The board thought it impossible that a Portuguese team could win that famous trophy and some sharp guy in the meeting said, "Make it 1,500 euros." So they did, and that was in the contract.

Guttmann loved money. Every time we had a big game, he demanded big bonus prizes for everyone in the squad. Maybe it was his way of motivating the players. His bonus payments were always twice the amount that the players won. So if we got 5 euros, he would get 10. That's why he tried hard to make us do what he wanted to do.

He was known as The Wizard and I don't know where that came from, but he was an excellent coach. The truth is that he was a bit superstitious as well: he always wore the same tie for every game. It was his lucky tie, the players thought.

He wasn't the only one being superstitious before the Barcelona game: my team-mate Domiciano Cavem, who was a defender, claimed after the final to have had a vision while he was sleeping a few weeks before the game. He said he had seen a strange figure telling him not to shave. If he obeyed, he was told, he would win the final. I have no idea if this was true or not, but the fact is that he was unshaven on the night of the game, which was unusual for him. I didn't ask why he was unshaven, because he was free to do whatever he wanted. And I am a quiet guy. Anyway, unlike Cavem, I had a night of perfect sleep in the hotel before the game. I never thought about the match when I was in bed, not for any game and not for this one.

We got a boost when we first walked out onto the pitch. There was a huge amount of support for us from the Portuguese immigrants in Switzerland. In fact, when we were on the pitch, we thought we were back in Portugal. There were so many people backing us that we felt that we were playing at Stadium of Light. It was a huge but welcome surprise for us.

I have to mention our goalkeeper, Costa Pereira, when I talk about the first goal that Barcelona scored. It was a bit... unnecessary, I think is the best way of putting it. But I didn't want to have a go at him, I thought it would be better to keep my mouth shut and not say anything. We wanted him to keep calm and did not want him to become more nervous than he already was. We just had to keep playing, looking to make some goals.

And in the end we managed to do that: I can't really remember the first two goals, but I do know that I didn't celebrate too much. As soon as their goalkeeper Toni Ramallets scored the second goal, an own goal, I just knew that I wanted the game to end quickly.

At half-time we were leading 2-1 and we were cheerful in the dressing-room. No-one was partying, because the game wasn't over, but you could see we all were very confident.

Ten minutes into the second half, I scored to make it 3-1 to Benfica. It was a great shot, from the edge of the area and it flew past the goalkeeper. I had a good eye for goal: when I first went to Benfica in 1954, I was a centre-forward. I was lucky that José Aguas had appendicitis at the time and he was having surgery. If it hadn't been for that, it would have been much harder for me to force my way into the first-team. I had started well, so when Aguas came back, the then-coach Otto Gloria kept me in the side as an inside-right. I kept my place in the side even when Guttmann came and brought Eusébio to the club.

As soon as the goal went in, my team-mates ran over and hugged me. I barely moved from the spot where I had struck the shot, because I was never expansive when I scored. It's the way I am, very quiet. But at that moment, despite there being over half an hour left on the clock, I felt that we were going to win that game and the European Cup.

But Barcelona had a great team and they attacked us a lot as the game wound down. We definitely had to suffer to get our hands on that cup. Costa Pereira was in better shape in goal. After his mistake early on in the game, he grew calmer and he did well to keep out their crosses and shots. He could do nothing to stop Zoltán Czibor scoring a late goal, but we held on to win the trophy.

It was an incredible feeling to lift the European Cup. I'd held a lot of trophies in my hands before, including the Portuguese championship trophy and the Portuguese Cup. But this was much bigger, much heavier, than any other cup I had ever held. We kept the party in the dressing-room. All the guys were partying, but there was no champagne. The coach didn't let the players drink any alcohol.

Guttmann was obsessed with discipline. Maybe that was the secret of his success. It was good to give us that discipline. If he hadn't done that, maybe we would never have achieved what we did.

The players were afraid of him and had a lot of respect for him. He would fine the players for the smallest thing. Once we were coming back to Portugal from a European game and we landed in Madrid to get a connection to Lisbon. We were free for a few hours and we were just waiting around for the flight. Mario Joao, one of the players, was thirsty and went to the bar to buy a Coca-Cola. Guttmann saw him and asked, "Who gave you you permission to drink that?" And he fined the lad the equivalent of 2.5 euros. It was a lot of money back then. Our monthly wage was 12.5 euros, so it was one fifth of his wage. You could see that Guttmann loved money by the way he disciplined us. Fortunately, I was never fined.

Only when we got back to Lisbon after the final did the club offer us a big dinner and we had a bit of champagne. Each player got about 125 euros for the victory. It was a lot of money: the same amount I had spent two years earlier when I bought a second-hand Volkswagen after I got my driver's license.

I will always remember that as the first big victory that Benfica achieved in that era. Benfica had already won the Latin Cup in 1950, but when we won the European Cup for the first time, I knew that it was an even bigger accomplishment.

The following season, we were once again European champions. Now Benfica started to have success in Europe, we got a lot of phone calls and postcards from girls who wanted to meet us. In Portugal during the 1960s, it was not easy for a player to escape from all the temptations. I don't know if my team-mates ever answered these girls. I just know that I never did. After any games we played abroad, there were always lots of girls waiting for us in the airport, throwing themselves at us, trying to kiss us! We had to be very careful. Guttmann was always advising us. He used to repeat that footballers should only have sex once a week. Nowadays I think that the discipline he imposed on us was a bit exaggerated, but I guess I can understand it.

The big change in 1962 was the arrival of Eusébio into the team. He had actually come to Benfica in December 1960, but there were some bureaucratic problems and he wasn't allowed to play for the club until the new season. So, although he was at Benfica for the 1961 final, his first European Cup final was actually in 1962.

The 1962 final was in Amsterdam and we were up against Real Madrid, the team whose run of trophies we had ended the previous season. They really wanted to get back to their dominant ways and they still had their great players Ferenc Puskás, Alfredo Di Stéfano and Paco Gento in the side. The opening of the game was hell for us: we were 2-0 down within 20 minutes, with Puskás scoring both. I was utterly convinced that we were going to lose the game. But nobody said anything, because Guttmann was the only one allowed to yell at us.

At half-time we had clawed it back and were only losing 3-2. That was when Guttmann made an important tactical change, telling Cavem to man-to-man mark Di Stéfano. So Cavem, who was also unshaven for this game, kept on Di Stéfano for the rest of the game. He did not allow him any room and barely gave him a kick of the ball.

In the second half, I scored the equaliser. It was a goal identical to that one I had scored one year earlier against Barcelona. I hit the ball into the corner of the net from a long way outside the area. It took the goalkeeper by surprise, but I knew what I was doing and was pleased when it went in.

A few minutes after that, we were awarded a penalty and Aguas was the man who usually took the penalties. The player who had been fouled was Eusébio and he was back up on his feet. When he saw Aguas picking up the ball, he stood up tall and asked me if he could take the penalty. I said to Aguas, "Let the kid take it, he's confident." And he did take it, and he scored.

After the goal, one of the Real Madrid players, Santamaria, called Eusébio a *maricon* (meaning, 'faggot'), but the younsgter didn't know the meaning of the word. He came over to me and told me what had happened. I said, "Next time he calls you that, call him *cabrao* (meaning, 'silly bastard'), and then he will be furious."

Sure enough, Eusébio ended up scoring our fifth goal and he did exactly that. He ran around the pitch yelling it with his arm raised. All my team-mates chased him, but I didn't bother because he ran too far!

Eusébio was from Mozambique, like me, but I didn't know him from there because he was only 12 when I went to Lisbon. I was 19. When I was in Lisbon, we didn't have much contact with the football world in Mozambique, but every time one of our players went there on holidays, they always came back mentioning Eusébio. He played for Sporting de Lourenço Marques, now Maputo, and all they would say is that he was "a great player who scored lots of goals".

We had also heard a lot about him from the coach of a Brazilian team called Ferroviaria de Araraquara. The coach, José Carlos Bauer, had played under Guttmann at Sao Paulo. And his team had gone to Mozambique to play against Eusébio's team. When Bauer next came to Lisbon, he met Guttmann, who asked him about Eusébio. "How good is this kid Eusébio, then?" he said. Bauer had no doubt. "Well, if I had the money I would buy him for my side," he replied.

The first thing Guttmann did the next day was to meet with the Benfica board and tell them to get Eusébio. The player's family only allowed him to go to Lisbon if he had a signed contract before he got on the plane. Benfica paid the equivalent of 1,200 euros in cash for a two-year contract. Eusébio was still under 18 and his mother had to sign a document saying that he couldn't play for any other team than Benfica. She didn't know how to write, so she just printed her finger on the document, which was signed by some witnesses. He started to play for the reserve team and there he stayed until Benfica solved all the bureaucratic problems, which came about because Sporting Lisbon claimed to have rights over him.

Guttmann knew that Eusébio was, had to be, a first-team player. The one who suffered most by that decision was Santana, who lost his place in the team because of Eusébio. He played at inside-left, with Aguas at centre-forward.

And so it was Eusébio who scored twice in his first European Cup final, a dramatic 5-3 win over Real Madrid. That Madrid side broke up after the game, as they were a lot older than us. Many of their players were over 30. Our youth had won the day and we managed to turn the result in our favour.

Some people claimed that Guttmann had doped his players, but that is completely false. If that had happened, Portugal would have been thrown out of the 1966 World Cup. We knew that there were some rumours from people outside Benfica who didn't believe us and were jealous. We always went to training camp with the team on Thursdays and Fridays and endured Guttmann's iron discipline. It would have been impossible to take something that he didn't approve of.

After the 1962 final, we were given a bear by a Dutch zoo. We took the bear to Lisbon and the person who grew closest to the bear was Guttmann himself. When we landed back in Portugal, we had to give the bear to Lisbon Zoo. We named him 'Benfica'. Every time any Benfica player went to the zoo, he had to see the bear. And there was always a Benfica fan, by the name of Agostinho, who spent all his time in the zoo, just watching the bear.

We had the same bonus payment for the 1962 victory, about 125 euros. Oddly, the highest prize we ever had was after the 1965 final, which we lost 1-0 to Internazionale after a mistake by our goalkeeper, Costa Pereira. Shortly after the goal, he had a serious injury to his spine and substitutions weren't allowed in football. So we had to play the entire second half with an outfield player, Germano, as our goalkeeper. Still, we didn't let in any other goals. Our chairman, Mauricio de Brito, came to the dressing-room after the game and said, "Lads, don't be disappointed. You may have lost the game, but you didn't lose everything. Your prize is 150 euros." I think it was more than we would have got if we had won.

I don't know what happened between Guttmann and the Benfica board after he won the European Cup in 1962, but he resigned from the job. I know that he was angry when he left. It is said that he launched a famous curse over the club, saying that Benfica would never win the European Cup again. And the truth is we were in the final on three other occasions in that period - in 1963, 1965 and 1968 - and we lost them all.

The 1963 final was our third final in three years. It was against AC Milan at Wembley. I had to hobble out of the game with an injury, after a clear foul by Giovanni Trapattoni. I ran past him but he chased me, fouled me from behind and broke my foot. We were 1-0 up, thanks to a goal from Eusébio, but there were no substitutions and we had to play most of the second half with ten players. We ended up losing 2-1, as José Altafini scored both of their goals.

I never spoke to Trapattoni again, not even when he was managing Benfica in the 2004-05 season. Nothing. I don't want to talk to him again. He meant to do that. After the game, an Italian TV station invited me to go to Milan to meet him on a TV show. They paid for my flights, my hotel and everything else. I went there to the studio, but Trapattoni never showed up. This proved to me that he really wanted to injure me. Otherwise he could have gone there and just said, "I'm sorry." But he chose not to.

Benfica went on to lose the European Cup final in 1988, against PSV Eindhoven. In 1990 they were in the final again, this time against Milan. Before that game, some board members went to Vienna to pray at Guttmann's grave. But Benfica lost again. 1-0.

They say it's a curse, but I don't believe it. I believe in God, not in the Devil. I think Benfica can win the European Cup again, because they are a great club. All they need is a bit of luck. And if that happens, I will celebrate more than I used to when I was a player.

SANDRO MAZZOLA
FORWARD 1954–1977

BORN   8th November 1942, Turin, Italy
SIGNED   1954 as Apprentice
INTERNAZIONALE CAREER   565 games, 160 goals
HONOURS   4 Italian League titles, 2 European Cups,
2 Intercontinental Cups, 70 Italy caps
LEFT   Retired, May 1977

Sandro Mazzola started his career in the spotlight; famous for being the son of former Italy international Valentino Mazzola, who was killed with his Torino team-mates in the Superga air crash of 1949. By the time he was 22, Mazzola Jr was famous in his own right, as an Inter regular and a key part of Helenio Herrera's double European-Cup winning side. He helped Italy win the 1968 European Championship and after his retirement, worked as a sports director at Inter before taking the same position at his father's former club Torino. He now works as a pundit for Italian TV station RAI.

Internazionale 3 v Real Madrid 1

Wednesday 27 May 1964

Prater Stadium, Vienna
Attendance 72,000

Inter win the first of back-to-back European Cups one year after AC Milan lift the trophy, confirming the dominance of Italian teams in Europe

Teams

Giuliano Sarti	1	José Vicente
Tarcisio Burgnich	2	Isidro Díaz
Giacinto Facchetti	3	José Santamaria
Carlo Tagnin	4	Enrique Pachin
Aristide Guarneri	5	Ignacio Zoco
Armando Picchi	6	Lucien Muller
Da Costa Jair	7	Amancio
Sandro Mazzola	8	Rafael Felo
Aurelio Milani	9	Alfredo Di Stéfano
Luis Suarez	10	Ferenc Puskás
Mario Corso	11	Francisco Gento

Mazzola 43, 76, Milani 62	**Scorers**	Felo 69

Referee: Stoll (Austria)

We were leading 3-1 and just waiting for the final whistle. It was like the clock didn't want to run. We all knew the game was over, we were about to win the European Cup for the first time, and against the great Real Madrid. It was an unbelievable feeling. I couldn't ever have imagined that.

Before the game, just outside Vienna's Prater stadium, I had seen Alfredo Di Stéfano. I stayed for a while, just hypnotised by him. All around it was dark, there was very little light. He looked so big. I think I looked at him for ten minutes without saying anything, just admiring this immense champion chatting with his team-mates. Here was my idol, just a few yards in front of me. I desperately wanted his shirt. So in the last minutes of the game, I ran alongside him so I could be the first to ask for his shirt. Even though his side were losing, Di Stéfano kept on fighting until the end. A real leader. But when the referee finally whistled, I realised how far away Di Stéfano was. Before I started to run towards him, Ferenc Puskás touched my shoulder. I turned around to him. "I played once against your father. Well done, boy, you honored his memory. You deserved that," he said. And he gave me his shirt.

My father was Valentino, captain of Torino, the team that was killed in the 1949 Superga air disaster. He was one of the best Italian players of his era. Immediately I forgot everything: the trophy, Di Stéfano's shirt, the celebration. My prize was there, given to me by an incredible player. I can't describe how I felt. Even now, that shirt is the most prestigious thing I have from my career. Sometimes I hold it in my hands and my memories immediately come flooding back.

It hadn't been so easy at the beginning of my career, when I was a teenager, because everybody who used to come to watch me play was expecting to spot a player as gifted as my father. But I wasn't. So the comments weren't always positive, and to be honest sometimes it was hard not to get depressed because most of the time I could hear people saying, "What does he pretend to do with the football? It would be much better for him to give up sooner rather than later."

Sometimes I felt lost, because I was the only one to really believe in my chances. At one point, when I was 16, I even decided to play basketball. But it wasn't for long, because football was my real passion. Paradoxically, it was only when I was a professional footballer that being the son of my father became something which helped me. It didn't take long to discover that my father's supporters soon became my supporters. Now, I was in front of a living legend like Puskás, and

Internazionale had just won the European Cup final. What a just revenge, what a sweet achievement.

That win wasn't important only for Inter, but it marked a sea change in European football. Just one year after AC Milan's win against Benfica at Wembley, Italian football had won again. And in the next five years there were two more wins - one each for Inter and Milan - and one lost final. Not bad for what the press still now calls *catenaccio*, a supposed strong defensive style of play. I really can't understand that word, because in Serie A, I remember Inter used to play 13 or 15 matches every season when our goalkeeper did not even touch the ball. We were always attacking and trying to score more goals. The same in Europe. The only difference was when we had to play against a better team, when we used prefer to stay back and wait for them. That's what happened against Real Madrid that night in Vienna. That doesn't mean that we couldn't score goals if we were playing badly. If you think about that final, we had five attacking players on the pitch.

When our coach, Helenio Herrera, had joined Inter in 1960, he was already called The Wizard for his innovative methods. Everything was new with him. He made his name at Barcelona, challenging the great Real Madrid for years. When he moved to Inter, he asked for Luis Suarez to be signed as well. Angelo Moratti, father of Inter's current president Massimo, agreed with the Argentine coach.

Herrera was a proud, self-confident, strong personality, a bit of a dictator. He never shared any of his decisions with the players. He didn't like to discuss his opinion, even with the older players. The relationship between him and the squad was always up and down, because we knew he was charismatic, but sometimes his tough attitude was difficult to accept. He liked to tell the Italian press that when he flew to Milan to sign the contract, around 5,000 Barcelona supporters had gone to the airport to bid him farewell. Later Suarez explained that it wasn't really true. The supporters had gone to the airport, but only because they had bad feelings towards Herrera.

His arrival was really important for Inter and for Italian football. He established new ways for teams to train, get motivated, and focus on their diet. He set up almost half of the professional training sessions that you see now. Before each game he wanted every player to make a short speech about the match. A sort of promise in front of our team-mates, a way to force us to take our responsibility. Every week there was the nightmare of being weighed. If you had put on just one kilo, you were fined. He was obsessed with these details. Herrera used to hang big signs on the dressing-room wall, which said: 'In football a player who hasn't done everything is nothing', or, 'Modern football is all about speed', or, 'We will win because we are the best. Is there anybody who doubts that?'

He also liked to change the routine before big games, or invent something new to ease the pressure. Before a game against Juventus, which gave us the first Italian title under his reign, in 1963, he decided to change hotels at the last minute because he was worried someone would try to poison us. The day before the Vienna final, he cancelled the last training session and took all the players to a lake close to the city for some fishing.

But I can't say that my early days with Herrera were easy. I joined Internazionale when I was 12 years-old. It was Benito Lorenzi, a former Italy international, who insisted that my mother let me play. She didn't want me to because of school. Our personal agreement was I had to study and only when I had done all my homework could I go to training. I risked my Serie A debut for that. On the Tuesday before the last game of the season in 1961, our coach Giuseppe Meazza explained that as a protest, Inter would play a young team against Juventus in the play-off final. Inter had already won the game, but the Italian Football Association had decided to replay it because there were too many players on the pitch at the end of the game. I was excited, I couldn't wait for the match. Finally I would be playing against John Charles, Giampiero Boniperti, Omar Sivori. The game was scheduled on Saturday afternoon, but as soon as my mother found out that I had three exams the same morning at school, she refused to let me play. I was desperate. I didn't know what to do. In the end, Inter's sporting director Italo Allodi explained to my mother that I could go to school in the morning and then a club car would pick me up and take me to Turin. It was the longest morning of my life. In Turin we lost 9-1, but I scored the first goal of my career from the penalty spot.

A few months later came one of the biggest disappointments. I was supposed to stay with the first-team. I was training all summer with them, but after a friendly against Varese, Herrera drew up a list of players to travel to Egypt for some friendlies. There were 24 players in that dressing-room and only one was dropped: me. I was shocked. Even though my father was one of the biggest players of his time, football was different to now from a financial aspect. When he died, we left Turin to live in a village close to Milan called Cassano d'Adda. We were a poor family and my mother had to be helped. So when I realised Herrera didn't want me, I asked to be sold on. I needed money, so I was ready to play in the second division to earn some. Inter agreed to sell me to Como but before the signature I was asked to play one last game for Inter's reserve team. I played well and scored two goals.

I didn't know that Moratti and Herrera were in the stands. Only a few years later, I understood that it was Moratti who made Herrera change his mind. One day later, Inter called me and I signed my first Inter contract. Within two weeks, I was a regular and my life had changed.

In a few years, Herrera had built a tenacious, disciplined, fighting unit. He always insisted you have to train the mind before the body. His training sessions were really hard, he couldn't stop and when we complained to him, he always used to answer, "The ball is not tired yet, let's keep going." He was a leader and no-one was brave enough to stand up to him. Only Suarez, who we called 'Herrera's son', could enjoy a special relationship with the coach.

Suarez was the perfect professional footballer. When I joined the first team, he was my example, he taught me so much about how to behave in the right way. He used to train on his day off, always eating and sleeping well. Maybe it was because they knew each other for a while but Herrera was always tough with us, and mild with him. I remember one night, we had just won a match against Real Madrid. It was a friendly but we were excited anyway. Herrera didn't want us to celebrate, so as soon as we were in the hotel, he sent us to our rooms. No party, no celebration. So disappointing. A group of players came into the room I shared with Suarez for a private party: champagne, cigars, poker. We were having fun. At one in the morning someone knocked on the door. It was Herrera, who came in and started shouting at us. While we were scared, Suarez kept on smoking his cigar. "Picchi, you are fined. Mazzola, you are fined. Corso, you are fined," he said the next day. All of us except Suarez. Someone went to Herrera asking why Suarez hadn't been fined. "Because he wasn't in the room," he answered. It was a lie, he had seen him but preferred to pretend otherwise.

I frequently shared a room with Suarez. Even now he is a good friend. He talked to me so many times about the great Real Madrid side, with Di Stéfano, Gento and Puskás that when we met them, I almost knew everything about them. Suarez liked to say how strong, skilful and fast Real Madrid were. They were idols before they were opponents. But the problem was, before that final, we were so scared and worried about being beaten that Suarez realised it was better to tone down his words.

Our first round game was against Everton. To be honest it was the toughest game of the run. We suffered so much. They were really a good team and we were not used to playing against a team who fielded two central strikers. I played pretty badly, I don't know why. But we won 1-0 on aggregate and got through. It was a great feeling because it was new for all of us. Inter had already won many national trophies, but it was the first time playing in the European Cup. We could feel the pressure because the year before Milan had won the competition, the first Italian team to do so. We didn't want to do worse than them even though it was not easy because we didn't know anything about our opponents, not like today. Herrera used to go and watch other matches and later he described the way they played. But we did not have any videos. Herrera always took care of the psychological points of the game.

So before every match he gave us a picture of our next opponent. "This guy will mark you, he will kick your arse all the time. Calm down and try to be as quick as you can be. He is strong but not as fast as you," he told me most of the time.

The European matches were exciting, and I loved travelling even though I was, perhaps understandably, scared of flying. The second round was against Monaco. The 4-1 score doesn't properly explain those two matches because they were battles. We won both games, but in Marseille, where Monaco used to play their European games, we had three injuries and were down to eight men for the last 20 minutes. At that time there weren't substitutes, so I played in defence after scoring two goals. It was a great feeling winning away. For me it was even more important because I scored my first European goals. At the end of the match the Monaco captain, a France international, came over to congratulate me. Such an honour.

In the quarter-final, we played Partizan Belgrade and they were probably the easiest games of the run. We hadn't any particular difficulty in winning the games. The night before the second leg, we all were in a hotel. As usual, Herrera wanted to check what we were eating and drinking. I always had problems with my digestion, I don't know why. Herrera's diet always gave me some stomach problems. That night I was chatting with some team-mates in the restaurant of the hotel when I spotted Suarez get up, take a knife and fork from the table and go to his room, which I shared with him. I couldn't understand the reason. After a while I decided to join him. I knocked the door, but there was no answer. I knew he was in, so I kept knocking. After a while Suarez opened the door. I came in but he was silent.

"What's going on here, Luis?" I asked.

No answer. But then I saw some bread on the table. Herrera had banned bread and Suarez was such a professional. In the end, he confessed. Then I realised why he always travelled with two bags. One was for his clothes, the second for the extra food. So it became our secret, a private agreement. We used to eat normally with our team-mates, only risotto with olive oil and sometimes beef. But after dinner, in our room, we had our real dinner, with French wine, bread, cheese and chorizo, for which Herrera probably would have killed us.

Despite us reaching the semi-final, we still never thought we would win the trophy. At least I never thought it. Everything was so new for me, I couldn't look too far ahead. My philosophy was to live day by day because we all knew that our lack of international experience could kill our dreams.

The semi-final against Borussia Dortmund was pure excitement, two great matches against a proud opponent. Germans never give up and Borussia were the same. I know there were some rumours about the referee: according to some journalists, the ref was paid to let Inter win. From my point of view, I have to deny that completely. We were a better team and the ref didn't give us anything. I can't understand all the speculation. We were a really strong team and we deserved what we got. We won 4-2 on aggregate. Only envy can explain those meaningless words.

To be in the final was enough for me. I was only 22. I would never have thought I could play at such a high level. Two years earlier I was ready to sign for a Serie B club just to earn some money and to prove to myself, and others, that I could be a professional footballer. And now I was going to play against the best team in the world. A team who had won the most important club competition five times in a row. Thanks to Suarez we knew almost everything we could about them.

Today, you can watch the big stars like Ronaldinho, Zinedine Zidane or Wayne Rooney, almost every day on TV. And after that, you feel you know them. But it wasn't like that in the past. Most of the time you were up against players you had never seen before - but not with Real Madrid. Di Stéfano, Gento, Santamaria and Puskás, they were all living legends. In my opinion Di Stéfano was the greatest of all time. Forget Pelé and Diego Maradona, he was superb and even better than them. Suarez told us about Puskás, 'The Colonel'. He explained that when Honved played, the Communist regime used to reward him for every international victory by upgrading his status in the Hungarian army, so finally he had really become a colonel. I couldn't wait to play them.

The night before the game I couldn't sleep. Herrera had felt there was too much tension in the squad and tried to calm us all down. I don't know if I felt we would be beaten, as at the bottom of your heart you always hope you can achieve the impossible. But Herrera was concerned that our nerves would stop us playing at our best. He had a sense of revenge for not being able to beat Real when he was with Barcelona, so he didn't want to lose this final.

Since he arrived in Italy he was seen as a good coach, but he hadn't won anything. Milan's coach, Nereo Rocco, had just won the European Cup, and the press liked to stoke the rivalry between them. They were two different personalities, two opposite characters. Rocco was almost a father to his players, changing clothes in the same dressing-room and confiding in his most experienced players, while Herrera was the boss, a bit cold in personal relations.

Herrera was a proud man and, even if he always denied it, this match was particularly important for him. He felt he had to prove something. He hadn't immediately won things with Inter. In fact, one year before the final he was almost fired by Moratti. The Inter president, at the end of Herrera's second season, was disappointed by the poor results and had decided to change coaches. His plan was to appoint Edmondo Fabbri and sack Herrera. Fabbri had already signed the new contract but when Herrera found out, he went to Moratti's office and made his point. He could be really persuasive and so, after one hour in the meeting, Moratti decided to renew his trust in Herrera. It was a good decision because that year [1962-63] Herrera won the Italian League, and the following season we won the European Cup. The only problem was for the players, who had two summer training sessions: the first under Fabbri, the second under Herrera.

But those kinds of matches, like a big final, are the easiest to prepare for as a coach. You don't have to spend too much time trying to find the right motivation. You are already sure all the players will give 110 per cent on the pitch. Your only concern is to use your advantages in the right way.

That was Herrera's main effort. Inter's style of play was quite simple in terms of tactics. We all knew what to do on the pitch. Armando Picchi was the *libero*, behind the line of defenders. The two centre-backs were Aristide Guarnieri and Tarcisio Burgnich. On the left side, Giacinto Facchetti was almost a winger. In midfield, Carlo Tagnin had the role to tackle and mark the most gifted opponents. On the right flank was Jair, on the left Mario Corso.

Suarez was the playmaker whose job was to create. I played alongside a central striker, Aurelio Milani, in attack. When Herrera was at Barcelona, his tactical system was an attacking 4-2-4. In Serie A he didn't wait too long to change that because in Italy it didn't work. You could say that we played 3-4-3 with almost five players with an attacking attitude. That's why I laugh every time someone accuses Inter of playing *catenaccio*. Of course, against a stronger team we preferred to wait and play counter-attack. But also we were a team who could score many goals and if you have the opportunity to watch one of our games, you can admire the fantasy and high quality of our football and you will never get bored.

As I said, the night before the game I couldn't sleep. I was in the room with Suarez. We had just finished our second dinner and we had a chat. I can't remember what we talked about. Suarez had more experience than me so he could deal with the tension better. At midnight he switched off the light and fell asleep. I can't count how many times I got out of bed. I slept for a few hours. All my thoughts were on Real Madrid. I didn't dream anything, not of scoring, not winning, nothing, even though before an important game you always hope something like that will happen.

Herrera made another change to our routine: he told us to get changed in the hotel. He didn't want us to spend too much time in the Prater stadium before the match. He thought we would be more worried if we were close to Real. Our hotel was our safety, our protection, so he preferred us to leave there only when we were armed for battle. It was another great intuition from The Wizard.

When we arrived at Prater, Real Madrid's players were already there. They looked calm, confident. We walked past them and went to the dressing-room. I stopped to look. I was so fascinated by them I couldn't stop watching them. Like a fan, I was there, just a few metres away. I don't know how long I stayed there. I only remember at a certain point Suarez went over me and woke me up. "Sandro, you will see them later," he said. "Don't worry, they are going to play against us. You can't miss them. But now, come to the dressing-room."

For me it was a dream come true. It's difficult to explain but just being there, playing against them, was an honour which I hadn't yet realised. In the dressing-room Herrera didn't give any particular speech. There was a terrific silence. No-one talked. I couldn't look at my team-mates' faces. I only looked at my boots while Herrera reminded each player of his duties. Usually he tried to increase our confidence. In this case, he didn't deny their incredible strength but he was sure with our pace and enthusiasm that we could do well. It would have been the last hurrah for Puskás and Di Stéfano.

In that season, the holders Milan overcame IFK Norrköping before having the misfortune to meet a fired-up Real Madrid in the quarter-finals. Real ran out 4-1 winners in the Spanish capital then lost 2-0 at San Siro, enough to earn a last-four clash with Zurich, who were beaten with ease. You could feel tension in the air.

During the warm-up, our goalkeeper Sarti saved a ball, but fell badly. He was so nervous he thought he had broken his shoulder. "I can't play, I can't play," he shouted many times over. Herrera called for the reserve keeper, Bugatti. He was sitting in the stands because back then there wasn't a bench. But Sarti's injury wasn't so bad, it was only the tension of the occasion that had got him worried. So, as soon as he realised he would miss playing the most important game of his life, he recovered.

In the first 20 minutes of the game, I don't think I touched the ball once. I was running around, but I couldn't do any good. A couple of times, Suarez came over and shouted at me to be more focused. After a while I calmed down and started to play better. And before the break we took the lead. Guarnieri passed me the ball and, despite being surrounded by defenders, I flicked out my left foot to fire it into the roof of the net.

I couldn't believe it. I never celebrated a goal too much. Maybe I'd point just one arm to the sky. But this time it was a totally different story. I was over the moon. So I started to run around, I couldn't stop. Soon Suarez joined me and calmed me down. "What are you doing? The game is not over yet." He was worried by Real Madrid's reaction and thought they might take extra motivation from my huge celebration in their search for an equaliser.

During the break no-one talked in the dressing-room. Again, only silence. Herrera said only a few words, suggesting that we play deep against them and hit on the counter-attack. To be honest, no-one still believed we could have won the game like that. We knew the second half would be even tougher than the first. It was true. A few minutes after the break, Real Madrid were dominating the game. They forced us to defend and we were lucky when Di Stéfano hit the post.

But after a counter-attack, Milani scored a second goal for us. Just at that moment, we finally started thinking we could win. And I don't know why, but for a moment I started to think about my father. I can't say too much about him because my memories only started when I was about six-and-a-half. I can't remember anything before then. My mind had probably erased everything from before. The first time I saw some pictures of him, I was so surprised because he wasn't really tall, but for me, when I was a child, he was like a giant. He had these hands, these big hands, which were for me a sort of protection.

For many years, I had a bad feeling towards Torino. For no reason, to be honest, but in my mind I couldn't forget that my father was dead just because he was playing for that team. It was a silly point but it was what I felt.

Many times I went to Superga Hill, where the plane crashed down, but never on the anniversary, when all the Torino fans go. Many years later, when I was appointed as Torino's sporting director, I decided to go there on that day. And I'll never forget what I saw. For the first time, I experienced the immense love that Torino supporters still had for my father, 50 years after his death. Superga is quite far from Turin, but despite that, hundreds of people make that walk to honour his memory every year.

Soon I was woken up by Real Madrid, who scored just a few minutes later through Felo. But at that moment we weren't worried any more. We knew we could, and in fact should, win the match. It was a unique opportunity to put our name in football history.

Seven minutes later, I had the privilege to score my second goal, after tackling Santamaria, and that gave us the trophy. At the end we were so happy, but too mentally drained to celebrate much. I only remember Moratti came onto the pitch. It was his win, overall, and we all knew that. He was a sort of father to me. He was the person who wanted me at Inter.

I couldn't forget when I signed my first contract. His secretary called me. I went to this huge office, just him and I. I was a 20-year-old guy, and very shy. Usually Allodi, the Inter sporting director, was in charge of this stuff. Moratti never discussed the player's contracts. But in my case he made an exception.

"Okay Sandro, how much do you want?" he asked me.

I really didn't know what to say, I was so intimidated. I just couldn't answer, so after a while he offered me 9 million lire [almost 5,000 euros] per year, which was really good money. But the surprise was even greater when he decided to give me an extra 4 million lire [2,250 euros] for the previous season.

"You weren't paid fairly last year," he explained to me.

He was generous. Before I played for Inter I had never bought a car. At the start of every season, his secretary used to call me saying there was a new car for me. I never asked for it, it was just up to him.

So when he came on the pitch we all ran over to him and put him on our shoulders and walked around the pitch. In the dressing-room, we couldn't stop admiring the trophy.

After my father died, my mother left Turin and went to live in a village called Cassano d'Adda. She got married again and that man had become a real father for me. He meant so much to me that at that moment he was the only person I really wanted there to celebrate with me. Moratti knew that and invited him into the dressing-room. It was anther special gift from the Inter president, and one of my most special memories of that night.

When we went back to Milan, there weren't any Inter supporters waiting for us at the airport. It wasn't common to do that in Italy, but we didn't mind. Even then, our hearts were still bursting with pride.

BILLY MCNEILL
DEFENDER 1957–1975

BORN   2nd March 1940, Belshill, North Lanarkshire, Scotland
SIGNED   1957 as Apprentice
CELTIC CAREER   831 games, 34 goals
HONOURS   9 Scottish League titles, 7 Scottish Cups,
6 Scottish League titles, 1 European Cup
LEFT   Retired, May 1975

Billy McNeill is the most successful captain in Celtic's history, winning 23 major trophies in his 18-year playing career in Glasgow. His relationship with coach Jock Stein exemplified the club's era of success and he followed his mentor as Celtic coach in 1978, winning three league titles in five years. After spells at Manchester City and Aston Villa, he returned as Celtic coach and won the Double in the club's centenary year. He is now a columnist for Scottish newspaper *The Scottish Sun*.

Celtic 2 v Internazionale 1

Thursday 25 May 1967

Estadio Nacional, Lisbon
Attendance 45,000

Celtic become the first British side to win the European Cup, and manage it with an all-Scottish eleven

Teams

Ronnie Simpson	1	Giuliano Sarti
Jim Craig	2	Tarcisio Burgnic
Billy McNeill	3	Aristide Guarneri
John Clark	4	Giacinto Facchetti
Tommy Gemmell	5	Gianfranco Bedin
Bobby Murdoch	6	Armando Picchi
Jimmy Johnstone	7	Angelo Domenghini
Willie Wallace	8	Sandro Mazzola
Steve Chalmers	9	Renato Cappellini
Bertie Auld	10	Mauro Bicicli
Bobby Lennox	11	Mario Corso

Gemmell 63, Chalmers 84	**Scorers**	Mazzola (pen) 8

Referee: Tschenscher (West Germany)

I can still see it now. It's the one moment I will always take with me from that game in Lisbon against the mighty Internazionale. I was standing just inside my own half and could see down the spine of the pitch. Bobby Murdoch hit a shot from the right hand side and Stevie Chalmers touched the ball past the Italian goalkeeper. It was something we had worked on with our coach Jock Stein, who encouraged the policy that front players should try and get on the end of any shots from distance that were struck. The forward was always encouraged to run across the line of the ball, and on this occasion, I could see it happening. Before I knew it, the ball was in the net and we were ahead; 2-1 up, against the favourites for the competition.

I can't really remember what I did next, I don't think I threw my arms in the air, but what I do know is that I have never run so quickly in all my life to go and hug Stevie. He hadn't started the season in the first team, so this was a great reward for him. One of the things that made our team great was the competition we had in the side and when Joe McBride, who scored a lot of goals for us that season, was injured, Stevie came in and did a great job. That is one of the reasons we won the trophy on an amazing day, but there are many others.

Jock Stein was the man that made all of our dreams come true and, more than anyone else, I owe my career to him. I would have continued the path taken by many young Scottish players into the English game had he not intervened. I was playing for Scotland Schoolboys against England and Jock was at the game, he was Celtic reserve and youth team coach at the time, and he liked what he saw. He basically forced the then-Celtic chairman Sir Robert Kelly to sign me for Celtic. There had been interest from a number of English clubs, but Celtic hadn't come near me before big Jock influenced the matter. It was 1957 and I was one of the lucky ones.

The first thing he did was send me for one year to a local junior side called Blantyre Victoria. Coincidentally, Jock had also played for them in his career, and like me as a centre-half. The reason I went to Blantrye was the same reason most people go there, as part of a toughening up process. One year spent with them taught you to appreciate how hard other people had to work to make it in football. I learnt an awful lot there: how difficult it is to play at that level, because after all I was only a boy playing among men, but I also learnt the benefits of listening to more experienced players and paying attention when someone offers you advice. These players may not have been amazing stars, but they had plenty of senior experience and were happy to help a young player just starting out. So you'd have been stupid not to listen to them.

Jock then left Celtic in 1960 and went to Dunfermline to become manager, where his side beat Celtic in the 1961 Cup final. He went to Hibernian after that, but returned to Celtic as first-team coach in 1965. He was the same man as he was before, but slightly different as a coach. He now had ultimate authority to do anything because he was the club's manager. He also now had the experience of working at Dunfermline and Hibs, so when he came back he used that well.

Jock changed everything at the club. The first thing he did was make everything - whether it was training, working, running or playing - something to be enjoyed. It wasn't like that before. It was old-fashioned, so training would consist of running around the track and throwing medicine balls at each other. We very rarely used a ball in training, but Jock changed all that. He allowed us to express our enjoyment during games and always told us to remember that the ball was the most important thing in football.

One of the most astonishing things about the Celtic side of that time was that we all came from within 25 miles of the Celtic Park stadium. I grew up in a mining town called Bellshill in Lanarkshire, and John Clark, my partner at centre-back, was also from Lanarkshire. Jimmy Johnstone was also from round the corner and the whole team had a bond because of our geography. We may not have all started out as Celtic fans, although I always was one, but by the end of that season, we were fans, and for life. John and I had played with each other in youth teams and the reserve team and there was a relationship that grew because we played so often in the same team.

We were both very lucky because when Jock first turned his hand to coaching in 1958, we used to travel in to training with him. There was a bus that went from Lanarkshire to Glasgow and the bus Jock took always was different to ours, it got to his stop before the one we took. It was funny though, if we were at the bus stop and Jock wasn't on the bus, we were not allowed to get on it. But if he was on the bus and we weren't there, he would stay on the bus anyway and never wait for us. We would always wait for him, but never the other way around.

We were only part-time then, and I was spending the rest of my time working surveying. But football was the big dream and I was doing all I could to make it happen. The club eventually gave Jock a company car and he used to drive us into work. On the way in we just used to listen to his stories, he would tell us about his career as a player at Albion Rovers and Llanelli in Wales. It was our reserve coach Jimmy Gribben who recommended him to Celtic and when he came to Glasgow he eventually became captain.

Before Jock returned to the club in 1965, Celtic were dawdling in the past. When he came back, it was like a breath of fresh air. He understood the younger players there and could bring out the best in them. He established discipline, but entertainment was always a part of it: he made everything fun, so when we got up first thing in the morning and were off training, it was with a spring in our step as we knew that we would be working with a ball. He revolutionised the club.

When we went into that 1966-67 campaign, I think very few people anywhere in Europe would have been able to name any of the Celtic players. But by the end they would certainly have been able to, even though our success was very much a team success, we all worked for each other. The team gave their all in every game, we simply didn't know how to die.

The bond really took root when we went on a tour for five and a half weeks to the United States in the summer of 1966. The year before, we had shown we were capable of doing well in Europe as we got to the semi-finals of the European Cup Winners' Cup. We played Liverpool and there was some controversy in that game. We won the first leg 1-0 at Celtic, but should have won by more. In the second leg, against a Liverpool side that were magnificent, we lost 2-0, but had a perfectly good goal chalked off and that still rankles. Some people still talk about it now, so that gives you an idea of how annoying it was for us. That indicated to us that we could achieve something that, until 1966, the rest of Europe hadn't realised. We had an appetite, we were a proud, determined, aggressive squad of boys that believed we could beat anyone on our day.

None of us had ever been to the US before and our relationships were really forged then and have never disappeared to this day. We played 11 games over there, including three times against Tottenham Hotspur, and we didn't lose a single game. So by the time we returned, we were confident about the season ahead and looking forward to a European campaign.

Our first match was against FC Zurich and we didn't know a lot about them. To be honest, it was more important for Jock to get us prepared properly, and he was good at that. The day before the game, he would go through the opposition and mark out how they played, the system, who were the better players and the ones we had to watch out for. But he didn't dwell on it, it was more important to him that we would go out and play well and show our ability.

We did that, beating Zurich 2-0 at home and then 3-0 away, thanks to two goals from Tommy Gemmell, our left-back. Tommy was a tremendous player who ended up scoring a fantastic goal in the final. But this team could score goals from all over the pitch, and Tommy was a great example of that. He loved attacking and Jock was happy for him to do so, as long as the time was right. But here was a left-back who not only scored two goals in that game against Zurich, but he scored in the first leg against them as well, our first goal of that European campaign. What's more, Tommy then scored in the final against Inter, and he scored again when we reached the final in 1970 against Feyenoord. To be a left-back and to score in two European Cup finals is an incredible achievement, but that was Tommy for you.

At that stage we were not thinking we would go on and win the European Cup, but we were doing well in the league and Jock had convinced us that anyone would find us difficult to beat if we all contributed and worked hard. Jock's theory was that everyone had to enjoy it and make a contribution, and if we all did that then that was all he wanted. No-one would kid us that we were the best eleven individuals playing in Europe, but on our day we could be the best team.

We beat Nantes in the next round, winning 3-1 in both of the legs. Jimmy Johnstone was excellent against them. He was a superb creative player, who was powerful, quick, strong, talented and game for anything. On his day he was unstoppable, but like many talented players, it was a question of finding when his day was. That was where Jock was so special: his man-management skills were excellent, he was brilliant at psychology and never asked players to do things that they were not capable of doing. How he treated wee Jinky is a good example of that: he knew that different personalities needed different treatment, so often Jinky would get an arm around his shoulder while the rest of us would get a kick up the backside!

We were up against Vojvodina Novi Sad in the next round, the quarter-final. They were a really difficult side, they were big, strong, powerful and with good ability that you expect from Yugoslavs. But for us, it was just another step on our great adventure. We lost the first leg 1-0 and that was the night that Real Madrid were knocked out of the competition by Inter: we barely registered that as we were focusing on our own progress.

The second leg was huge and we were goalless at half-time. Jock was not worried and told us to keep working hard. We had players like Bobby Murdoch and Bertie Auld in midfield who were both superb creative players, and our front men could also create and score. In the second half, Tommy crossed and Stevie Chalmers equalised.

The score was at 1-1 on aggregate and we were approaching the end of the match. In those days, if the tie was level there would be a play-off game which could have been difficult. But then we had a slice of luck, a great ingredient which everyone wants - and it's amazing how it often comes to those who deserve it!

We had a corner and we had practised a routine on the training pitch. I often went up for them and did score some important goals. I had scored in the Cup final against Dunfermline in 1965, which helped us win Celtic's first trophy for seven years. As I said, we had people all over the team who could contribute with an important goal, so it wasn't a surprise if one of us did pop up and score, especially with the good crossers we had in the team.

So when this corner came in from Charlie Gallagher, I had already made my run and seen that their goalkeeper was coming for it, but he had misjudged it and I knew I was beating him to the ball. My header was a high one and it went over the man on the line and in.

I did not appreciate how late in the game it was and I felt that there was some time still to go. I turned to John Clark and said, "Come on, let's make sure we don't lose this now." He looked at me like I was crazy and said, "Billy, it's finished. It's all over."

I said, "Come on John, it's not over until the referee blows his whistle. Let's just concentrate and get to the end." I thought there were five minutes or something left, but the fact is, the Vojvodina players barely had time to exchange passes from the restart before the referee blew for full-time.

And that's where the luck comes in. Yes, you can try all game to score a goal, but when you get one like that which comes so late, like with only seconds left to play, you have to say there is luck involved. Maybe the goal came about in part because of slackness on their side in defence, but to manage to score the winner in the last minute is a big slice of luck. It was a huge excitement for us to be in the semi-finals.

So the adventure continued and we used to live for that draw on a Friday. We used to crowd around the radio at training and through it would come. We always looked forward to the next game just because we were pleased to be in that round, and we never looked at other teams or examined other parts of the draw. So when we drew Dukla Prague in the semi-final, we did not dwell on the sides we had avoided, Inter and CSKA Sofia, instead Jock just made us focus on the Prague game.

Jinky put us ahead in the first leg of the semi-final at home, but they equalised before Willie Wallace, a terrific player who had only joined that winter, scored twice to win it 3-1. He could play from midfield and link up with people in front of him.

Then came the second leg, which is the one game I don't think any of us look upon with satisfaction other than the fact that it got us to the final. We could always defend because no team is ever successful if you leak goals, but our greatest strength was the fact we played open attractive football with skilful front players who could stretch defenders and score goals. Our ultra-skilful players were Jimmy Johnstone and Tommy Gemmell but others, like Bobby Murdoch and Bertie Auld, were magnificent ball-players. We would be described as a creative team that could defend.

But against Dukla Prague, it was the only game in which we adopted a more cautious approach. I've never been sure whether it was an intentional thing or something that just happened. Maybe it was because in the early part of the game, our backs were to the wall, but we did get more opportunity to express ourselves as the game went on. But it was hard early on and we put in a defensive performance, however unexciting, that was totally foreign to us.

The Prague team were quite old and were reliant on Josef Masopust, a wonderful player who I had played against for Scotland, when he played for Czechoslovakia. It wasn't easy to get to know players back then, as the TV was not so prominent, so the manager had to go and investigate and he would come back to tell us how they would play. But with Masopust, lots of us had played against him.

Right at the end of the game, when we were delighted that the 0-0 scoreline had got us through to the final, he was reluctant to shake hands with any of us. We moaned about it at the time, as we were not that impressed. But then there was a knock on the dressing-room door and Masopust came in to apologise to us.

"I am sorry about that," he said. "It's just that I was so disappointed not to win the game as I know now that I will never play in another European Cup final again." The fact that he came back and apologised to us elevated him tremendously in our eyes.

But we were through to the final and for us it was a massive achievement. Four days after that game we played Aberdeen in the Scottish Cup final, which we won 2-0, and then we held Rangers to a draw at Ibrox, which won us the league title. All those things going on were great for us because it kept the focus on the games in Scotland and not on the final, which was to be against Inter.

But of course we were excited about the final and the build-up to the game was perfect. Once again, it was another step on this wonderful adventure we were having. And our next stop was to be the final in Lisbon.

We didn't know anything about Inter then. Names didn't mean anything to us, we knew they were full of Italian internationals, and Italian teams were always worthy of great respect. I think they were the hardest challenges you had in those days, but they took some of own ability away because of the methods they used. I often think that the style of football they played, *catenaccio*, should have been foreign to the manner in which the Italian nation lives. Everything they do in Italy is with panache except in football, but when they had the ball they could play and keep it. If they had adopted a different, more flamboyant style, I think that they could have won even more.

Anyway, it later emerged that their coach Helenio Herrera was thinking of leaving to go to Real Madrid and their most expensive player Luis Suarez was also thinking about a return to Spain. We knew none of that at the time, though, and just went to our retreat in Ayrshire, a place called Seamill, where we spent a good week preparing for the game, relaxing, and having a laugh.

We knew this was a different game to any other we had played in: for a start, there were TV crews from all around the world who were coming to film us and do interviews. Every day another player would be picked out for an interview, and this was unlike anything we were used to, but we were enjoying it. It was the biggest game of our careers, but the team had the belief that we could beat anyone on our day.

The more time we had to think about the game, the greater the excitement that built up. Jock had found us a great hotel in Estoril to stay in and we went there two days before the game.

The weather was great, but we took it easy. On our first day there we were sat by the pool and Jock announced to everyone: "Okay lads, none of you should spend more than half an hour sun-bathing today please. If you spend more time than that in the sun, it will tire you out for tomorrow."

Obviously that put a positive thought in all our heads: we didn't stay in the sun, which was hotter than we were used to, so we all presumed that we would therefore not be tired for the game the following day. It was typical Jock psychology, but it worked. I've often wondered since whether sitting in the sun does actually tire you, but if Jock said it, we all believed it. He planted that idea in our heads and it had the desired effect. We all felt fresh for the game.

And we had a feeling that we could beat anyone. We were very aggressive, and very fit. Jock laid down great importance on fitness, he believed the fitter you were the more expressive you could be with your own ability. We were proud of our achievements so far, and our fitness and ability. We had an attitude that allowed us to expect to win if we played well enough. I'm not saying that we went out to Portugal thinking we were going to walk all over Inter, but we were determined to make sure they knew they were in a game.

Herrera tried some gamesmanship before the game, promising to put on some travel arrangements for Jock to go over to Italy to watch Inter play, but that never materialised. They also claimed that they had the lucky dressing-room, but you can imagine Jock was unimpressed with that. So the Herrera aspect never entered our thoughts, although their games were clear when there was a toss-up for the dug-outs and the Italians jumped in for the one that had been designated to be ours. But Jock stormed over to the dug-out and toughed it out with the Italians to ensure that we got that dug-out. It was a small victory, but I think that one-upmanship helped us in the match.

The night before the game, there was a Scottish lad who had opened a golf club in Lisbon and he invited us to his house. England were playing Spain in an international friendly and we watched the game and walked back to our hotel just after ten o'clock in the evening. It all seemed perfect, we got back to the hotel, had a laugh and a cup of tea and then went to bed. I can't even remember if I slept badly that night, but I just wanted the game to come around. When the next day came, it just flashed by. All our thoughts were about the game.

By then we had realised that the Celtic support was special, but the atmosphere before the game was something else. The Celtic fans, it turned out, played a huge part in the game. They were there when we arrived in Estoril, and they were there when we got to Lisbon. Bear in mind that this was before the days when it was easy to hop on a plane to zip round the continent like today - these people had saved their money and come to support us. They had gone down so well in Portugal and impressed the local hosts that we felt the Portuguese fans also wanted Celtic to win.

Jock was very detailed about the opposition on the day of the game, but the biggest emphasis he placed was on our own performances. He believed that if we gave of our best, we could do it. He thought we could win it.

I was captain of the side, but I didn't give a team-talk before the match. Jock wouldn't allow you to do anything like that. To be honest, it was an easy group of boys to be captain of, as we'd been together for such a long time and relationships were good.

If there was any aggression, it was permitted: I mean, if I felt like having a go at any of the players, that was allowed, but it took longer for new players to come into the side and start bawling out team-mates. There was a seniority, but the rows never got out of hand and were always dealt with quickly. We were like the old Labour party, we argued amongst ourselves, but no-one else was allowed to get involved.

I'd been captain quite often in school teams and had been made captain of Celtic before Jock came back to the club. I was appointed skipper in 1963, and I always enjoyed the responsibility. I moved into it quite easily and if you have good players alongside you, it's easy to be a captain. Unfortunately, my responsibilities were off the pitch as well, and that was the more difficult part, trying to keep people in line when they were enjoying themselves. We did enjoy ourselves, and that was part and parcel of the harmony that was in the squad. It was a great bunch of boys.

I will admit that there were some nerves in the tunnel before the game. As we lined up opposite the Italians, who all looked very smart in their strip, there was more tension than anything else. That's when Bertie Auld started singing a Celtic song at the top of his voice and we all joined in. You should have seen the looks on the Italian players' faces. I don't think they'd ever heard anything like that before.

Coming onto the pitch was incredible, I can remember seeing the stark contrast in the difference in the teams' colours. Inter were wearing blue and black and we were in green and white, there was a brilliant contrast in the stands and our travelling support was massive.

But the game did not start well. We lost the first goal to a penalty kick when Jim Craig was judged to have brought down Cappellini after eight minutes and Mazzola scored. We thought the penalty was an injustice. As it turned out, it helped us because it gave us even more motivation. As we were behind, there was only one thing we could do and that was to get hold of the ball and to put them under pressure.

This was the biggest game any of us were ever going to play in and we wanted to take advantage of it. When we lost the penalty we were a bit aggrieved as we thought it was a wrong decision. Since then I have seen the challenge again and it was the right decision, it was a penalty. But at the time we felt we had been robbed.

We dominated the rest of the half and were surprised at how well their goalkeeper Sarti had played. We had him down as a weak link before the game, but he just kept out everything we threw at him: and the way we were playing was the way Jock had always told us to. Our attitude to the game was an exciting one, we wanted to entertain people and we enjoyed our football as well. That was all going on out there, we were playing good football all the time.

At half-time we were still behind and words were exchanged as we walked to the dressing-rooms. It was a very long walk, you had to go underneath the ground and down a long tunnel before you got to the dressing-rooms at the end. We gave the referee, who was from West Germany, a bit of stick along the way. I don't know if he understood English, but by the time he got to his room, his ears must have been red.

Jock talked about the situation sensibly at half-time. He was very calm and he said that if we had a grievance against the referee, there was only one bunch of people who can do anything about it, and that was us. I think that helped us, it focused our mind, and Inter didn't even have a shot in the second half.

Still Sarti kept keeping everything out, but we just kept plugging away. There were times when I thought, 'Oh no, this is just not going to be our day. Don't tell me it's going to be all over, we have had 80 per cent of possession and we're going to go home with nothing.'

I have to mention the fans again: there was great support, but what was interesting is that it came whenever we needed it. It was almost telepathic. There were times in the match where we were hammering away at them, but getting nowhere, but when the fans felt like we needed encouragement, it came.

By the time Jim Craig cut the ball back to Tommy Gemmell just after an hour, Bertie Auld and Tommy himself had already hit the woodwork. But Tommy struck this shot just perfectly and it screamed into the net. It was relief more than anything when he scored, but I knew then that it was going to go our way.

Then Stevie Chalmers scored the winning goal with six minutes left, and I expected a really tough end to the game, I thought we would have our backs to the wall but that never happened. They were gone, beaten. It was down to the fact that we had put them under so much pressure during the game that they couldn't believe it when that goal went in. I think they had nothing left in the tank.

When the final whistle went we had no idea what to do. We had not even talked about it and it was all quite chaotic. Obviously we were delighted, but also totally shattered. But I do have regrets: I still think of that when I watch Champions League finals and I would love to change what we did after the game.

We were essentially a team - that was where our success had come from - so I thought it was only fair that rest of lads should be involved in the presentation of the trophy. But when it happened, Jock was talking to the press and the players were celebrating so Sean Fallon, who was Jock's assistant coach, and I walked across the pitch to pick up the cup. But even now I wish that we had all been there. We should all have been there.

By the time I got back into the dressing-room, it was a complete mess. I never got any memento from the game, which is a shame. The rest of the boys had gone into delirium, we knew it was massive being the first non-Latin side to win the European Cup and the way we had done it - with such exciting football, and with a team of local boys - had been impressive. There was an official presentation dinner after the game and there was talk that the Italians would not come because they were so shattered by the defeat. But they turned up, although they were not very chatty.

The whole realisation of what we had achieved did not register until we got back to Glasgow and saw the tremendous reception that was waiting for us. I remember thinking it was going to be special on our return when I looked up at the crowd after the game. All our wives were there, but I also saw my next-door neighbour. He was not a big football fan, but I saw him waving at me as I left the ground and that brought it home - even non-football fans were there to support Glasgow. The fans lined the route from the airport all the way to Celtic Park when we got back and that was tremendous.

To this day, we still get a massive appreciation from the fans of Celtic. It could have happened again, but that's in the past now. We reached the final in 1970, but instead of being the under-dogs against Feyenoord, we were the massive favourites. There were a whole lot of factors that worked against us that season: our season had finished earlier than the Dutch season and they were actively fighting for the title. The biggest problem was that we got carried away thinking that our semi-final, against Don Revie's Leeds United side, which was the best in England at the time, was the final. We got a bit complacent after that and maybe disregarded the ability of Feyenoord.

We lost that final 2-1 and that is a huge regret of mine. I dearly wish we could have won that game to add to our victory of 1967. But still, it was a privilege to have been part of that Celtic side, and my team-mates from then are still my friends today.

ALEX STEPNEY
GOALKEEPER 1966-1978

BORN 18th September 1942, Surrey, England
SIGNED August 1966 from Chelsea; £55,000
MANCHESTER UNITED CAREER 534 games, 2 goals
HONOURS 1 English League title, 1 FA Cup, 1 European Cup,
1 England cap
LEFT Transferred to Dallas Tornado, July 1978

"The single most important factor behind our championship success in 1967 was signing Alex Stepney," said United coach Matt Busby. One year later, Stepney was lifting the European Cup, following a performance in the final, when he saved a late chance from Eusébio, that secured him hero status in Manchester. After 12 years at United, he moved to Dallas Tornado in the North American Soccer League and played for non-league Altrincham before retiring in 1980. He now works as a pundit for TV station MUTV.

Manchester United 4 v Benfica 1 (after extra-time)

Wednesday 29 May 1968

Wembley Stadium, London
Attendance 100,000

Manchester United become the first English club to win the European Cup

Teams

Manchester United		Benfica
Alex Stepney	1	José Henrique
Shay Brennan	2	Adolfo Calisto
Nobby Stiles	3	Humberto Fernandes
Bill Foulkes	4	Jacinto Santos
Tony Dunne	5	Fernando Cruz
Pat Crerand	6	Mario Graça
Bobby Charlton	7	Mário Coluna
David Sadler	8	José Augusto
George Best	9	Eusébio
Brian Kidd	10	José Torres
John Aston	11	Antonio Simoes

	Scorers	
Charlton 53, 99, Best 93 Kidd 94		Graça 75

Referee: Lo Bello (Italy)

We were the first English side to play in a European Cup final. There were five minutes left of the game and the score was 1-1. I remember a ball was played from deep within the Benfica half and I knew that their striker Torres was being marked by Bill Foulkes. But I could see there was a huge gap where Eusébio was running through. Nobby Stiles was meant to be marking him, but he'd shaken him off. I thought the ball was coming into the box so I ran off my line. I guessed that I was favourite for the ball, but it did not quite work out like that.

The game was at Wembley and we had an undoubted advantage because most of the neutrals there were supporting us. But the grass at Wembley was very lush, and that slowed the ball down. As soon as I realised that the ball had slowed, it was clear Eusébio would be getting there first. He was one-on-one with me and in that split-second, I decided to stop and take a few steps back. My first thought was that he was going to chip me - I was so far off my line that there was enough room for him to do that - but then I remembered that Eusébio was the type of player who always wanted to burst the back of the net.

So I stood up straight, and told myself not to dive down. This guy had the hardest shot in football and I was about to find out about it. He smashed the ball straight at me. It thudded into my chest. We played with a Mitre ball in those days and I always said afterwards that the make of the ball was imprinted backwards on my shirt! I admit that it hurt me.

I was good at stopping shots, although it wasn't something we worked on specifically in training. I was lucky to have the co-ordination to hold the ball into my chest after I made the save. Sometimes keepers can't react quickly enough to a shot from close-range, and they block the ball, but the rebound comes out and is put away. I am still convinced that if I had dropped the ball, Eusébio would have scored what would have been the winning goal.

I didn't have time to think about the consequences of my save. I was a goalkeeper that always looked to throw the ball to a team-mate, so as soon as I got the ball, I threw it out to Tony Dunne on the left wing. He was in space, and I wanted him to start a counter-attack.

It was a baking-hot evening and by that stage of the game, we were all exhausted. It was over 90 degrees in the stadium and all of us were shattered, on both sides. The Wembley pitch sapped the energy out of us. It was the last game on the turf before the Horse of the Year show and that always ruined the pitch, so the grass was slightly longer than usual. The Portuguese players may have been used to the warmer climate, but the pitch sapped their energy as well - even though nine of their players had played at Wembley for Portugal in the 1966 World Cup semi-final against England. They lost that game very late on as well.

So when the 90 minutes was up, we were shattered by the prospect of another 30 minutes to play. We knew that whoever scored first in extra-time would go on and win the game. The other side would be so deflated by it, so that's what we were going for.

The funny thing is, the second goal we scored only happened because all our players were so tired. I picked up the ball three minutes into extra-time, and rolled it to Dunne again. He didn't really want it, he was so tired, so he passed it back to me. It was the days when you could pass back to goalkeepers, so it wasn't a problem for me to pick it up and try again. I rolled it to another defender, Shay Brennan. But he didn't want it either, as he was so exhausted. So there I was with the ball again, with no-one to pass it to.

So I kicked it as far as I could down the pitch, and Brian Kidd flicked it on. Out of our whole team, George Best was the fittest of the lot and he was the only one still running around. He ran onto Kidd's flick-on and got past Mário Coluna before rounding José Henrique in their goal and passing the ball into the net. That lifted all the players, they were suddenly full of running again. Benfica, as we had thought, were totally deflated. We scored two more goals in the next five minutes.

Brian had matured a lot during the season, and that game was played on his 19th birthday. He had played in every game in our European campaign, though Matt Busby, our coach, had brought him in for a few weeks in the league and then took him out again and told him to work hard and keep improving.

It was his performance in the semi-final that had got us to Wembley in the first place. We were drawn to play Real Madrid in the semi-final and won the first leg 1-0 at our place. Bestie had scored against them and we went over there confident that we could do enough to get to the final. But once we were in Madrid, it just wasn't happening for us.

We weren't playing well. I've no idea why, it was just one of those games where nothing seemed to be working. Denis Law was the captain, but he was out with a knee cartilage injury. So Brian played. We were in real trouble in the game and before we knew we were 3-0 down, and 3-1 down on aggregate. In the last minute before half-time, one of our boys played a hopeless ball into their box and Brian chased it down. It was only because he was a young lad and had the energy to go after it, to be honest. There was nothing on and no-one else in the side would have bothered. But he managed to make their centre-back, Ignacio Zoco, nervous. He headed the ball back to his keeper, Betancourt, who himself had run out to claim the ball. Zoco ended up heading the ball into his own net, and suddenly we were only one goal behind.

Matt sat us down at half-time and told us to relax. "Come on boys, why are you so nervous?" he said. "You are all great players, just stop worrying so much. We can get another goal here and if they score as well, we can get another one on top. Just go out there and play the game. Go and enjoy yourselves."

And though we hadn't played well in the first half, we went out and played well in the second half. David Sadler pulled another goal back and Bill Foulkes made it 3-3 on the night, which was basically the winner for us. We were in the final.

That game was particularly emotional for two of the players on our side: Bill was one and the other was Bobby Charlton, who was captain of the team in the absence of Denis. They were the only two survivors from the Munich air disaster, a crash that had happened ten years earlier, which killed 22 people including seven of the 'Busby Babes', young United players set for stardom. Busby had also survived it.

I was only 15 at the time of the crash. I remember coming home from school and hearing about it. I was living in London at the time and obviously I knew it was a tragedy, but I never imagined I would later be part of a United side, least of all playing under Busby himself.

I had started my career at Millwall and had won three caps for Alf Ramsey's England Under-23 side when Chelsea came in for me in the summer of 1966. When I signed for them, their manager Tommy Docherty had told me he was selling Peter Bonetti, who was the Chelsea number one, to West Ham. I was looking to become a first-choice goalkeeper in the First Division, so I moved to Stamford Bridge. But a week after I moved, the Chelsea chairman Joe Mears had a heart attack and died. It was the day after England had beaten Norway 6-1 and he was in Oslo at the time. A new chairman came in, and said, "Bonetti is staying."

So I was stuck on the sidelines and United, who had a pretty poor start to the season, came in for me after seven games. We recovered to win the title in my first season there. That was how we qualified for the European Cup in the first place.

I had only been at Old Trafford for just over a year when the European Cup final came along, but the feeling among those people who had grown up at Old Trafford, and had spent more time there than me, was that they thought this campaign was Matt Busby's last chance. United had lost a great team at Munich, but it was a tragedy that happened during a European Cup campaign. So to be in a European Cup final itself was already very emotional.

But no-one said a word about that. It was never spoken about, we never brought it up and nor did Matt, nor Bobby, nor Bill. It didn't enter our heads as a matter for discussion. We just all got on with our jobs.

Matt was a very laid-back sort of guy. He wouldn't hide behind closed doors, he gave good advice and encouraged us to play attractive football. He gave us freedom to play and wanted us to enjoy ourselves out on the pitch. That was important to him. When he named the team, he would always announce it to us and I think he enjoyed that aspect of it: selecting the team was for him like a jigsaw puzzle, and he had to fit all the pieces in the right place.

And he was a master-mind when it came to working with young players. Brian was the perfect example: there were lots of young kids waiting in the reserves and youth teams and one was always going to come through. That was Brian and he took his chance when he got it, that's for sure.

Before the Benfica game, Matt singled out just one of our players, which was rare. He said to Nobby Stiles, "I want you to man-mark Eusébio like you did for England in the World Cup semi-final." Well, Nobby marked him, but he didn't stick to him like he did two years earlier - that save I had to make at the end of the game is proof of that!

Two years earlier, United had beaten Benfica 5-1 in Portugal in the European Cup quarter-final. I wasn't at the club then, but Best had scored twice. His surname said it all. It was such a shame what happened to him, and a real pity that there was not the same kind of coverage of football then as there is now. You see archive footage of the same goals now, but the truth is, some of the things he did were incredible. He played off-the-cuff, he was an entertainer and he always thought about the defenders he would be up against and came up with new ways of tormenting them. He did not just create goals, he once scored 33 in a season and the ratio of left foot, right foot and headers was pretty even, I think. There haven't been many players before or since who could do that.

We had gone to the United States on a tour before that 1967-68 season and played Benfica in a friendly in Los Angeles. They won the game in LA 3-1 with Eusébio scoring two penalties. So we knew a bit about them and weren't bothered when they won the toss to wear their home strip at Wembley. We were wearing blue kits, they were in red, but that did not affect us.

It was my dream as a kid to play for my country and win the FA Cup final at Wembley. Those were the two best things I thought I could do in football: to go to United and win the First Division title was a bonus; to be part of the first English side to win the European Cup final was also a fantastic achievement; and I am proud of that save I made from Eusébio. As soon as I made the save, he came up to me and acknowledged that I had done well. I have spoken to him since and he said he congratulated me because it was a great save.

The most incredible thing happened when the referee finally blew for full-time. When you win a final, most players will celebrate by going to their nearest team-mate, they will have a hug and celebrate together. But I have looked back at the game on video and all the players immediately rushed to Matt Busby. That was not rehearsed. He was such a great man, and it must have been in everyone's subconscious that it would mean so much to him.

I'd only been a professional for four years and this was something that I had never dreamed of. The highlights of the day for me were making that save, lifting the trophy for the first time, and running to celebrate with Matt after the final whistle, thinking, "We've done it for him." I remember that somehow my brother got in the dressing-room to celebrate with us. This was the pinnacle of playing football.

It was more emotional for Bobby Charlton, who was one of the Munich survivors. We were all staying at the Russell Hotel in London, and we had a big get-together with all the players and their families. But Bobby went to bed. He was absolutely exhausted. The next day, four of us were called up for an England friendly in Germany. Bobby, John Sadler, Nobby and myself went off to join the squad, so we all missed the homecoming in Manchester. That was upsetting.

After that high, it was inevitable that there would be some lows to follow. One year later, Matt stood down and Wilf McGuiness and then Frank O'Farrell came in. My old boss at Chelsea, Tommy Docherty, was appointed in 1972. I remember the following season we went to Spain for a pre-season tournament. We played Penarol of Uruguay and the game went to penalties. I ended up saving one and scoring our fifth one from the spot to win the game! That was how I became our penalty-taker the following season. For a brief spell at Christmas, I was joint-top scorer with Lou Macari and Sammy McIlroy with two goals! We were relegated that season, but came back up straightaway, and even reached the FA Cup final. I had achieved my dream, but we lost to Southampton and I had to wait for the following year to win the FA Cup, after we beat Liverpool in the final.

I always hoped that United would win the European Cup again, but I don't suppose anyone really imagined that it would be over 30 years later. Still, it took the club another 26 years to win the First Division title after we last did it in 1967. I was at the game between Bayern Munich and United in 1999, and it was just incredible. What a finish that was. I was also in Lisbon for the group game in the 2006 Champions League campaign, when Benfica beat United 1-0 to knock them out. It was the first time the clubs had met since the European Cup final and I guess it was about time Benfica won a game against us.

Even now, I am sure that fate played a big part in our success. You have to believe that. Think about it: of the two survivors from Munich, it was Bill who scored the winner in the semi-final against Real Madrid, and then Bobby who captained the side in the final because regular skipper Denis was injured and in hospital. And yet it was never mentioned. In a way, I can see why that was. Everybody who was involved in the Munich air crash is entitled to their own memories and no-one wanted that to change. But it was on my mind, that's for sure.

JOHNNY REP
FORWARD 1967-1975

BORN 25th November 1951, Zaandam
SIGNED 1967 from ZFC
AJAX CAREER 97 games, 41 goals
HONOURS 2 Dutch League titles, 2 Dutch League titles,
1 Intercontinental Cup, 1 French League title, 1 European SuperCup,
2 European Cups, 42 Holland caps
LEFT Transferred to Valencia, July 1975

Johnny Rep was 21 when he scored the winner in the 1973 European Cup final, which should have been the spring-board for his career. It turned out to be his highlight. He made Holland's squad for the 1974 World Cup, but like at Ajax, he struggled in the shadow of team-mates Johan Cruyff and Piet Keizer. He played in the 1974 and 1978 World Cup finals, losing both games, but still holds the Dutch record for World Cup finals goals with 7. He moved to Valencia and then became a cult hero at Bastia and Saint-Etienne. He now works as a scout for FC Omniworld, but would love the chance to work again at Ajax.

Ajax 1 v Juventus 0

Wednesday 30 May 1973

Red Star Stadium, Belgrade
Attendance 89,484

Ajax win their third straight European Cup final, the first team since Real Madrid to do so. To mark the achievement, they are allowed to keep the famous trophy

Teams

Heinz Stuy	1	Dino Zoff
Wim Suurbier	2	Silvio Longobucco
Barry Hulshoff	3	Sandro Salvadore
Horst Blankenburg	4	Giuseppe Furino
Ruud Krol	5	Gianpiero Marchetti
Johan Neeskens	6	Francesco Morini
Arie Haan	7	Fabio Capello
Gerrie Mühren	8	Franco Causio
		(sub. Antonello Cuccureddu)
Johnny Rep	9	Roberto Bettega
		(sub. Helmut Haller)
Johan Cruyff	10	José Altafini
Piet Keizer	11	Pietro Anastasi

Rep 5	**Scorers**

Referee: Guglovic (Yugoslavia)

There was a giant headline in Dutch newspaper *De Telegraaf* the day after I had decided the European Cup final with my header. It read *Goudhaantje*, meaning 'Goldenballs'. Earlier that season, the name had been given to me by Sjaak Swart, the team-mate whose place I took in the side. Swart was in his 30s and coming towards the end of his days as a footballer. He slowly saw me replacing him, which was tough for him. He had been in the first team for most of his life. Often when I replaced him, he saw me scoring important goals while he sat on the bench. That made him sigh and call me *Goudhaantje*. More and more people started to call me that. A reporter from weekly magazine *Panorama* who had a soft spot for me nicknamed me *Pietje Bell*, meaning 'Little Scamp'. He thought I was the kind of guy who would set loose mice in church. Okay, I was a bit naughty, but I never did that. I wasn't the one who would take the initiative to sneak out and party during our training-camps. Of course, we went out after we played, as a distraction. But if we had to play within three days we certainly didn't go out. Especially me. I knew I couldn't handle that. But I never got rid of those nicknames. They haunted me for the rest of my career and beyond. They left a huge mark on me.

I joined Ajax in 1967 when I was 16. I was playing for ZFC in Zaandam, my native town, who were in the Second Division. I was quite a talent. Even at 16, I had already played several times for the first team. My family loved football and one day my uncle, who was a good player himself, approached Ajax president Jaap van Praag to tell him he knew a nice little player that Ajax might like. They came to see me and offered me a place in their youth academy. At first I wasn't very pleased. It hadn't been a dream of mine. The youth academy wasn't as famous as it is now. I was paid by ZFC, although not very much, and at Ajax I had to drop back into the youth system. Anyway, I did it.

After a short time at Ajax I went back to my old club to play in the Second Division for another year. However, I was talented so Ajax approached me over and over again and convinced me to come back and stay in Amsterdam.

That was in 1969. I started to realise how much I wanted to get to the top. That ambition increased after a bus trip with a group of youth players to Paris where we saw the European Cup quarter-final play-off match in which Ajax beat Benfica 3-0 in the Colombes Stadium. Those were the sort of games I wanted to play in! I finished at the youth academy and when I was 19, Stefan Kovács promoted me to the first-team squad. I was the only player who moved up from the youth academy to the seniors at that time.

In my first season, I had a hard time keeping my head above water. It was hard to find my niche surrounded by such great players. I wasn't the only young player who was in the squad. Gerrie Kleton, Arnold Mühren and Johan Neeskens were my contemporaries. Neeskens was even younger, but he immediately won a place in the first team. I had played with him in youth games when he was playing for Second Division side RCH. I recommended him to Han Grijzenhout, my youth coach at Ajax. That's how Ajax discovered him. I wasn't jealous of him for getting in the first team. He was a different type of player, more mature than I was. I was just a 19-year-old forward and was competing for a place with Johan Cruyff, Piet Keizer and Swart.

After a while I found my level. I had prepared properly for my first season. It was 1971, the year after Ajax had won their first European Cup. I got back early from holiday and trained by myself. Of course I watched Ajax play again and again. Every now and then it was amazing, but sometimes it was sleep-inducing. I never forgot the fans in De Meer stadium making snoring noises when they were bored and wanted the team to play a bit faster. They were endlessly passing the ball back and forth, which was characteristic of Dutch football at the time. Tactically it was great, but it wasn't pretty for the fans. But once Cruyff or Keizer got things going, amazing things would happen.

We were a team of friends as well. I remember a match against Feyenoord when a rival fan was hitting Keizer with a flag-pole. All the players jumped off the bus to give him a beating. That was typical. I am convinced that I was already good enough for the team in my first year. I had proven myself in friendly matches and with occasional substitute appearances. I was fast and had an eye for goal, but Swart was 33 and still going strong. He was a great player, and part of a forward line that played together for about ten years. Imagine how unique that is. Nowadays clubs are lucky to keep teams together for two or three years.

On top of that, coach Kovács didn't have the guts to drop him. Meanwhile I was getting itchy feet. I had little playing time, but whenever I was given 30 minutes I always scored. The time had come for me to play every match. Or else I wanted to leave for another club where I could start and show my skills every week.

Kovács was a nice man. He allowed the players their freedom. He spoke on the same level as us and let us decide things. The players were in charge of discipline rather than him. That often got me, precocious me, into trouble. Once, I had a problem with Cruyff during training and it turned into a fight. It was a group of players who punished me: they did not let me play in the first-team or even sit on the bench for a month. That 'suspension' cost me a place on the bench for the 1972 semi-final against Benfica, which we won 1-0. It could be quite tough and the younger players were kept on a tight leash. Cruyff was really all over us and sometimes it was hard to accept. There was a lot of kicking, yelling and swearing. But maybe my pushiness deserved that punishment. My behaviour was caused by frustration at not playing and being criticised non-stop.

Except for these odd bust-ups, I had a good relationship with Cruyff. I learned a lot from him during training and in matches. We dovetailed perfectly on the pitch and he provided me with lots of assists. I know he often whispered in Kovács's ear to bring me on. Kovács understood football. I did not play under Rinus Michels at Ajax, but I noticed that many players saw Kovács as light relief in comparison. They had more fun. I played under Michels during the 1974 World Cup and thought he was tough, but with a good sense of humour. Back then, Ajax did not really need a coach. We just needed somebody who could hold the group together, who was smart. But there were times that Kovács gave the players too much freedom. It wasn't for nothing that he left after only two seasons.

On the other end of the scale, Michels occasionally went too far with his discipline. Keizer wasn't on speaking terms with Michels until he left Ajax. I don't think their relationship had any influence during the 1974 World Cup. Keizer didn't play the final against West Germany, but that wasn't because of the issues between him and the coach. Keizer had played against Sweden earlier in the tournament, but personally I think he was past his best by then. After the World Cup, he got in trouble with the new Ajax coach, Hans Kraay, and then he ended his career. That 1974 squad had three good wingers in the side - Rensenbrink, Van de Kerkhof and Keizer. I got along fine with Michels then. He wasn't too strict. After every match we were allowed to have a beer in the hotel.

Meanwhile I kept on fighting for my place in the Ajax first-team. In the Intercontinental Cup final second leg, I came on as a substitute for Sjaak Swart and scored twice. Thanks to those goals, we beat Independiente of Argentina 3-0. That was my career highlight to date, those two goals in a capacity Olympic Stadium. I remember both goals so clearly, as if I scored them yesterday. The first was a tap-in from a cross from Cruyff. Earlier there was an identical situation, but my shot hit the post.

The second goal started with a pass by Cruyff from midfield. I ran at full speed, beat the goalkeeper and slotted the ball home with my left foot. It was a beautiful goal, a typical example of why Cruyff and I worked so well together. When he made the pass, I was already at full speed to run onto it. Journalists told me that I said to Cruyff, "Just give me the ball and I'll score." I don't remember that, but it was typical of something I would say.

I was only 20 and I thought I had proved myself. My name was famous, but I still wasn't a starter. It was a major blow that one week later, I was playing with the reserves in front of 200 people. I got frustrated, and got unnecessary yellow cards for pointless fouls. In other games, I was sent off. And still I had no idea that this was going to be the most successful season of my career. Swart was still established in the side and Kovács was having problems replacing him. Just before the winter break I finally appeared in the starting line-up. It must have been the board or Cruyff who forced Kovács to bring me on. I was a different type of player to Swart. I wasn't a real winger, but more like a second striker. Neeskens and I were the perfect players to dive into the gaps that Cruyff created.

That second season, I almost finished up top scorer in the Dutch league. I will never forget who was top: Cas Janssens and Willy Brokamp. They both scored 18 goals, not that many. I scored 17, but only played 20 games. Imagine if I had been playing from the start of the season. I might have got 25 or 30 goals. It was a great year. We won the European SuperCup, the League title, the Intercontinental Cup and the European Cup. It was only after 1973 that the rot set in. From then on, it was downhill.

I did not score in any of the European matches until my goal in the final. I didn't start the first games against CSKA Sofia, which was in the second round. We won 3-1 and 3-0. I finally started against Bayern Munich in the quarter-finals. At home we completely outplayed them. It was 0-0 at half-time, but we won 4-0 and it could have been 8-0. I don't know why I didn't score. I played okay, but I guess I didn't get the chances.

We played the away game without Cruyff, which was weird. It was a strange situation. It was reported that Cruyff was injured, but nobody knew what was going on. He just didn't appear at the airport. We talked about it among the players. At the time, we were close to dislodging him as captain. We were still good without Cruyff, but we lost 2-1 to Bayern, who had Franz Beckenbauer, Sepp Maier and Gerd Müller in their side. I hit the post and had a goal disallowed.

So we were in the semi-final against Real Madrid and it was a highly-charged affair. They were a bit over the hill, and we managed to beat them. They scored a late goal at our place, but we still had the advantage at 2-1. At the Bernabéu, they put us under pressure, but our goalkeeper Heinz Stuy kept us in it with some great saves. He was notorious for letting in some easy goals, but more often saved the day for us. We won 1-0 in Madrid, with Gerrie Mühren scoring the only goal. He also wound up the home players by juggling the ball ten times while the Real stars just looked on. We didn't realise what a big deal it was at the time, but the world was amazed. We never spoke about it afterwards, for us it just didn't seem like much.

So we were in the final for a third successive time. But our preparations were a complete mess. We had the usual morning training on the Monday in Amsterdam, and then left for the airport to go to Yugoslavia. We arrived late on Monday and were staying in a huge hotel in Belgrade near the river. The players' wives joined us. They were staying on the floor below. My wife didn't come to Yugoslavia, because she was in the late stages of pregnancy and wasn't allowed to fly. I had dated her since I was 17 and we married at 21. That's the reason I never knew how popular I was with women. I was the only player with a fan club. A girl from Heemskerk had set it up. I just had to occasionally answer some questions.

Unfortunately our hotel was full of Italian supporters. They made a tremendous noise. As always, I shared a room with Gerrie Kleton. But all I remember is the noise. We could have had a better preparation. On the Tuesday, we had normal training in the stadium. I did not think too much about the circumstances. It was my first final and I was focusing on myself.

During the bus trip to the stadium I had a huge stomach-ache. That's what happened to me before every important match. That season, the matches against Bayern Munich, Real Madrid and Juventus - and the games to decide the league - were so close to each other that I must have had a permanent stomach-ache. But the pain always disappeared as soon as the game started.

There were more Italian fans in the stadium than Dutch ones. That made sense as Italy is not too far away from Belgrade. The atmosphere wasn't intimidating though. It was a pretty warm night. The pitch was in bad shape, very bumpy.

My direct opponent in the final was Silvio Longobucco. I don't remember anything much about this guy, so he can't have been a butcher with a knife between his teeth. Later in my career, I had more problems with Claudio Gentile. He was a few years younger and was more unscrupulous. The only reason I remember Longobucco is because there is a picture of me jumping with him as I headed in the game's only goal, and his name is in the caption. I jumped really high. I tower over him in that picture. I can still see that cross from Horst Blankenburg fizzing through the air after five minutes of the game. I just leapt as high as I could and the ball struck my forehead. I didn't make perfect contact, but the ball ended up in the back of the net. I was going for it, but it was lucky in the sense that it went perfectly into the corner . Dino Zoff, their goalkeeper, could do nothing about it. He wasn't just any No 1, he was superb and still only about 30 and played for another ten years after that. He was even a World Cup winner with Italy in 1982. I still have that picture of Longobucco and me in a friend's scrapbook and occasionally I go and look at the picture. When the ball went in, I celebrated as I normally did: just a simple recognition, with one or maybe both arms in the air. I get really annoyed when players celebrate with all their stupid dances moves these days. Act normal!

The crowd didn't see one of the best ever finals, but I don't agree with all the criticism that came afterwards. It may not have been a great final, but I have seen about 20 other awful finals since. The 2005 final between Liverpool and AC Milan is how it should be, with excitement from the first to the last minute. It wasn't even our fault in 1973: Juventus just didn't do anything. I think they were afraid of getting their arses kicked. We took an early lead, so we didn't need to do anything but wait for them. And they didn't want to lose 5-0, so their caution made the match boring. They had some chances in the second half, but I never understood why they played like that. Maybe they just couldn't do any better.

They did not have a bad team, though. As well as Zoff, they had Fabio Capello, Roberto Bettega and José Altafini. There was a moment in the second half when I really got involved. Altafini, who was about 35, broke clear and I said to myself, "I can't let it happen that they equalise my goal!" So as they were trying to score, I ran back as fast as I could. I will always remember how I slid in to tackle Altafini and break up that attack.

When the final whistle went, we were happy, but we weren't going to whoop it up. I changed shirts with Longobucco, but I didn't keep his shirt. I didn't keep any of the shirts I received down the years. I gave them all away. I regret that now.

When I look back, I guess many players thought it normal to win the European Cup. There was less joy compared to their first win two years earlier and also to the second, against Internazionale in Rotterdam. But for me, this was the first time. I could not wait to put that cup in the air and I loved walking around with it. I didn't even notice that not all of our players were doing a lap of honour.

The celebrations were pretty tame. We went to a casino. We bumped into some of the Juventus side there. I spoke to Helmut Haller, who had played for West Germany in the 1966 World Cup final against England. Then we had a party in the hotel with the players' wives. I felt even more excited about the win since I had scored the only goal. People still remember me in Italy. When I'm on holiday at Lake Garda, people point me out and talk to me about that game: not just elder people either, but younger fans too. They are much more into their football than in Holland.

The press was all over me. Queen Juliana invited us to the Royal Palace back in Holland. I have been there several times in my career. I can't remember if we were honoured at the theatre at the Leidseplein in Amsterdam as usual. We definitely were one year later with the Holland team. I especially remember our visit to the Catshuis, the Prime Minister's official residence, after the 1974 World Cup. That was great. It was spontaneous, the weather was great and we did the conga with PM Den Uyl leading the way! We had a party the evening before as well.

Everybody important in Dutch politics showed up, including Bernhard, the Prince of the Netherlands and Wim Duisenberg, the president of the Dutch Bank. Our reception at the Palace in 1973 was more low-key.

Looking back it was the end of an era, the last throes. Nobody could have imagined what would happen afterwards. I certainly didn't. The transfer market allowing players to move to Spain had opened and Cruyff left for Barcelona. That was the biggest loss for Ajax. He wasn't someone you could just replace like that.

It all happened in the pre-season of the 1973-74 season. We were at our training-camp in Drenthe, in the north of Holland, and there was a power struggle between Cruyff and Keizer which led to a leadership election. Most players were fed up with Cruyff and his whims and fancies and voted Keizer to be captain. Cruyff was the leader on the pitch anyway, with or without the armband. But when he lost the vote, Cruyff grabbed the phone and called Cor Coster, his father-in-law, who was also his agent. He went to Spain.

There was a story that Cruyff used to give me bad passes on purpose to show me up at not being able to control the ball. There was one match where I played awfully and the fans were booing me. I don't know if Cruyff did it on purpose or I was just having a very bad day. But I wouldn't put it past him to try and pull that sort of trick.

That season George Knobel had taken over from Kovács as coach. It didn't work out great. Knobel had joined us in Belgrade before the final. He watched the training sessions from the sidelines. It was a weird situation, although we knew that he would be our coach. After Kovács, who was so easy, we needed someone to play the tough guy. But Knobel wasn't strict either. He came from the south of Holland and it was hard for him to adjust in Amsterdam. For a southerner it was hard to cope with the mentality of the Ajax players. He was a nice guy, but Ajax wasn't the right place for him. He could not stop the squad falling apart. He arrived at the wrong time. If he had succeeded Michels in 1971, he would probably have two European Cups on his CV.

Without Cruyff, and with a whole bunch of bad purchases, the season was lost. We went out of Europe 2-1 on aggregate in the second round to CSKA Sofia, a team we had thrashed the previous season. It was an emotionally-charged game that we lost in extra-time, not helped by me missing a penalty at the end of the first leg. It hit the inside of the post and stayed out. Had it gone in, we would have won 2-0 and probably got through. The only highlight of that season was beating AC Milan 6-0 in the SuperCup. I scored one goal.

Not only were we missing Cruyff, but subconsciously the players had lost their ambition after three straight European Cups. New players like Willy Brokamp and

René Notten struggled to fill the boots of Cruyff and Mühren. Ajax made some unlucky buys. Then Knobel got fired after making unwise comments in an interview. He said Ajax were failing because the players were drinking and womanising. He used the wrong expressions: he should have said the players were past their best and trying too hard!

Hans Kraay, who had problems with Keizer, succeeded Knobel. Keizer called it a day, more poor purchases followed and the great Ajax era was definitely over. As so often happens, three golden years were followed by a long, dark period. The players were fed up. I was very young but I had already won every possible prize.

After two terrible years, I left Ajax as well. My Hungarian agent got me a move to Valencia, where the technical director was a countryman of his. In the past I was linked to AC Milan, Bayern Munich and Real Madrid, but none of those deals was ever concrete. When Michels followed Kraay at Ajax, there were rumours that I would go back too. I didn't have a good start in Valencia, but I stayed. In the end, I had some great times in Spain, together with Mario Kempes, one of the greatest players I ever played with. My time was over when I got into trouble with the President. I did not want to spend the rest of my contract sitting on the bench because the 1978 World Cup was on the way. I had to play.

So I went to Bastia, a small French club that was booming at the time. You have to be lucky when you make a move like that and I was. They were third or fourth in the league the previous year and every UEFA Cup match in Corsica was a carnival. When we won, fans fired shotguns into the air to celebrate. Before each league match, some guys stood behind the goal and fired their guns. It was intimidating for our opponents. We did not win everything, but we won a lot.

My best time in France was with Saint-Etienne, who were the biggest club at the time. I played with Michel Platini, another great player. I had the time of my life there and was very popular. A band called Mickey 3D even wrote a song and named it after me, because I was the lead singer's idol. The club recently invited me back and the fans were singing the song.

The good times ended because of tax fraud. The players who had received money under the counter were hit with big bills from the tax department. If that hadn't happened I would have stayed there, because my family and I felt at home. I continued my career in Holland, playing for Zwolle, Feyenoord and Haarlem. Then I ended my career. I had some problems with the coach, Hans van Doorneveld and I wasn't fit. I returned to ZFC, now an amateur club, and played until I was 41.

Looking back, I don't think I got the recognition I deserved. I got some publicity because I was a striker, but there were other players like Wim Suurbier, our full-back, who were marvellous as well. I made some important goals and played a major role in the team, but the presence of players like Cruyff and Keizer took away from my performances.

My nicknames also put a stamp on me for the rest of my life. They may be the reason I never became head coach of a professional club. People still link me to mischief and mucking around. It kind of fits the picture. 'Goldenballs' and 'Little Scamp' belong to me. I have had talks with clubs, but unfortunately have never been lucky enough to get a job. I never understood why Ajax did not want me as a youth coach. I've put my coaching ambitions aside now. I would only take a job if some club from the United Arab Emirates knocked on my door. I do some scouting for FC Omniworld now, a new team in professional football, and I like what I do. In the future, I would love to do that for Ajax as well.

I realise I belong to a generation who achieved something unbelievable, but I'm not recognised as much as before. Fame can be really annoying. We became living legends and I accepted that. But at the time it was harder and I was sometimes a bit too reckless.

Looking back on my career, I don't think I scored enough goals to become a real legend, like Cruyff. If I had helped Holland win the World Cup in 1974 or 1978, it might have been different. In those finals, I had some chances to score, to make myself immortal. If I had put them away, I would have become a real legend.

FRANZ ROTH
MIDFIELDER 1966–1978

BORN   27th April 1946, Memmingen, Germany
SIGNED   1966 as Apprentice
BAYERN MUNICH CAREER 322 games, 72 goals
HONOURS   4 German League titles, 3 German Cups, 3 European Cups,
1 World Club Championship, 1 European Cup Winners' Cup, 4 Germany caps
LEFT   Retired May 1978

Franz 'Bulle' Roth was a fierce and powerful midfielder with an ability to man-mark
opposition playmakers out of the game. He was spotted by a Bayern scout aged
20 and immediately won a place in the side. He kept that place for 12 years, as
a crucial part of the most successful side in German football history. Roth scored
in two of Bayern's three European Cup final wins but retired in 1978, two years
after the team began to break up following the 1976 success. He opened a sports
shop in Bad Wörrishöfen, near Munich, and still works there every day.

Bayern Munich 1 v Saint-Etienne 0

Wednesday 12 May 1976

Hampden Park, Glasgow
Attendance 54,864

Bayern win their third European Cup in as many years, but the game marks the end of the club's cycle of success, and Bayern has to wait another 25 years before winning the competition again

Teams

Sepp Maier	1	Ivan Curkovic
Johnny Hansen	2	Pierre Repellini
Hans-Georg Schwarzenbeck	3	Oswaldo Piazza
Franz Beckenbauer	4	Christian Lopez
Udo Horsmann	5 ·	Gerard Janvion
Franz Roth	6	Dominique Bathenay
Bernd Dürnberger	7	Jacques Santini
Josef Kapellmann	8	Jean-Michel Larque
Uli Hoeness	9	Patrick Revelli
Gerd Müller	10	Hervé Revelli
Karl-Heinz Rummenigge	11	Christian Sarramagna
		(sub. Dominique Rocheteau)

Roth 57	**Scorers**	

Referee: Palotai (Hungary)

The week before the 1976 European Cup final was pretty bad. We had drawn two games in the league and knew that we wouldn't win the championship. Our arch-rivals Borussia Moenchengladbach, who were coached by our old boss Udo Lattek, were running away with the Bundesliga trophy yet again. That hurt us.

To make matters worse, I was injured. I had an inflammation of the Achilles tendon and it simply wouldn't settle. I had a feeling that I wouldn't be able to play against the French side in the final. I was very anxious, even a little depressed. Bernd Dürnberger, who was an important player for us and had been outstanding in the campaign, looked doubtful too. Fortunately, our medical department worked wonders and got us both fit just in time.

We were staying an hour outside Glasgow at this lovely country hotel, Turnberry, on the Scottish coast. It had a wonderful golf course and we were looking at these old chaps in their chequered trousers driving their buggies and thought, "Maybe we should try that as well." None of us had ever been golfing before, but somehow it did the trick. We calmed down and relaxed a bit.

The worst problem for us was that we did not know where we stood. In the league, things had not gone according to plan, but in the European Cup, we had played well. All that goes out of the window in a final. It's 90 minutes and you need to have a good day to win. There's no second chance once you cross that line. So despite the fact that we had won twice in a row in the two previous years, we were very nervous. I remember that two Rolls-Royces were parked outside the hotel: the Rolling Stones were staying there. Some of us went to hear them practice. Mick Jagger said, "You'll do it." And we did.

It's funny when I think back to how it all started. I come from this small Bavarian town, Memmingen, and for young boys there was nothing to do after the war. All you could do was play football in those days. Fifteen to 20 of us would kick a ball around on pitches without grass, every day of the week until the sun went down. We constantly ran up and down. It was so much fun. It became even more fun when I was able to turn this hobby into a job and actually get paid for it as well. Is there anything better in the world than doing what you love doing and making money that way? I don't think so.

I was playing in the lowest league, it was called the C Class back then, with Kaufbeuren. It was an amateur side. We came up to the Bayernliga and after one year, Bayern Munich noticed me. They said, "You don't need a trial, Roth. We will watch you twice, once at home, once away."

They did, and then they made me an offer. It was 1966, just after the World Cup. Obviously, I signed straight away. You just have to try something like that, even if you're not so sure you actually have what it takes. Coming from an amateur side into the Bundesliga, you can't know whether you're good enough. But I had the ambition and the drive to prove wrong all those doubters in Kaufbeuren who had told me that I would never make it. What I didn't know is how fast things would work out.

I remember Sepp Maier, Franz Beckenbauer and Gerd Müller coming back after the World Cup in England to our training camp at the Ammersee. We had already been there for ten days. They were asking our coach Zlatko 'Tschik' Cajkovski about the new signings and he said to them, "Boys, I have somebody here with the power of an ox."

Maier said, "No, in Bavaria, we say 'bull', not 'ox'."

And that's how I got my nickname, 'Bulle'. It stuck.

In my first game with Bayern, against Frankfurt, I sat on the bench. But in the second, in Düsseldorf, somebody was injured and Cajkovski let me play wide on the right. From that moment on, I always played. It was unbelievable that it had worked out so quickly, but my physical power and doggedness made it possible. It was a fairytale. And it got better.

In my first season, we won the German Cup. Then we somehow managed to win the European Cup Winners' Cup in our first ever European campaign, even though we had a very young and inexperienced team. I scored the winning goal in the final against Rangers in Nuremberg. It was in extra-time, in the 108th minute. The ball came over the top and I was falling as I hit it, so I was only able to hook it towards goal. It went over the goalkeeper and into the net - but I never saw that. When I got up, I was surrounded by my team-mates. Cajkovski said to me, "Bulle, you are the king." That night, I went to bed with the Cup.

In 1969, we won the league title. Our new coach Branko Zebec was a disciplinarian and his tactical approach brought incredible results. From the first to the last day, we were always leading the table. And we only used 13 players all season. It's hard to believe but true. We had the makings of a great team, but in Europe, we ran into a Saint-Etienne side that was on fire. We had actually won our home leg 2-0. But in France, 40,000 fans made a frightening noise and we were hammered 3-0. Zebec went soon after. He had fallen out with some of the players, but I was not one of them.

I enjoyed playing football so much that it never mattered who the coach was. I got along with every coach I ever had because of this mentality. Maybe that was one of the reasons for my success. I was never the most technically-gifted player, but I gave everything and ran as far as my legs would carry me. I think my fellow players always appreciated my fighting qualities. Perhaps not in training, though. Uli Hoeness said he was always wearing shin-pads in training for fear that I would kick him across the pitch. In those days, he would often not wear them in matches. But we trained very hard and to be fair, Uli gave as good as he got.

I never had any problems with anyone. I was not a rebel like Paul Breitner and I was down-to-earth. I got married only two years after joining Bayern and my family gave me the strength and the security that I needed. I was always happy to switch off when I got home, but soon my son started asking, "Daddy, why did you lose today?" and then you could not help but have a discussion. Thankfully, we never lost too many games in those days.

In the Bundesliga, we were peerless. We won three championships in a row, in 1972, 1973, 1974. But in Europe, Ajax of Amsterdam were the most powerful force. There was no real rivalry with them because they were in a class of their own. We were always looking up to Ajax. They were winning everything with a sensational team and a sensational Johan Cruyff. But it wasn't him alone, they had a very strong unit. That was their big plus. As a young team, we were looking at them and hoping that we could catch up with them: one day. We trained for that all year, we were dreaming of one day holding the European Cup in our hands. We may have already won the Cup Winners' Cup, but the ultimate ambition was the European Cup. Every footballer dreamt of that.

So in 1973, we met Ajax in the quarter-final. They thrashed us 4-0 in the first leg in Holland. I have never been beaten like that. I had to mark Cruyff so it was doubly painful for me. Our goalkeeper Maier was so upset that he got up in the middle of the night and threw his shoes, shirt and shorts out of the hotel window and into a small canal.

In the return leg, we beat them 2-1. We knew they were still too good for us. But there was a sense that they might be at end of their cycle. Some players had left and their team was not quite the same, whereas we were staying together as a team and kept growing. We were hoping that our time would come, that we might be able to take over from them. Thankfully, it happened that way.

In those days, it was very tough to win the European Cup because only the league champions of every country got the chance. It was hard to get in and then you would face the best teams in Europe in straight knock-out competition. There was no room for error because you were not sure you'd be in the competition again next year. Naturally, you also needed a bit of luck.

There was no particular secret to our success. First of all, we were playing with virtually the same team for five, six years. That would never happen these days. That was key. We were getting better all the time. There was an instinctive understanding and it really helped that we were all from Munich or nearby regions and we shared the same mentality and love for the club. We were living it. We totally identified with Bayern, 100 per cent. In Maier, Beckenbauer and Müller we had the three best players in the world in their respective positions. They were the spine of the side.

Then there was Hans-Georg Schwarzenbeck, the enforcer in midfield. He was my room-mate for 12 years and everyone called him 'Katsche'. All the squad players were pulling together as well. The younger guys like Karl-Heinz Rummenigge wanted to show their ability. Bayern had a good team hierarchy, everybody watched out for each other. Individually and collectively, we developed a formidable team. We had a wonderful team-spirit and if you were down, Sepp would always pull a prank in the dressing-room and cheer everybody up.

We had this unbelievable urge to win the big trophy. If our coach Udo Lattek had told us to play two games every day, we would have done it. We told ourselves every game, "Come on, we have to do it." You need to be strong-willed and have a lot of heart if you want to achieve great things. Otherwise, you won't be able to go beyond your limits and get to 120 per cent of your capabilities. Ironically, though, we came close to getting knocked out in the first round in the 1973-74 European campaign in Sweden.

Atvidaberg, the Swedish champions, were a relatively small team and perhaps we took winning for granted after beating them 3-1 in the Olympiastadion. But they surprised us and won the second leg 3-1 to force extra-time and penalties. We just about scraped through. Conny Torstensson, their best player, wore red shoes that day and was so special that our president Wilhelm Neudecker decided to sign him after the game. Conny was very fast and skilful. He became an important player for us only a few months later, especially in the European Cup. He scored four goals to take us to the final against Atletico Madrid in Brussels. You were not cup-tied in those days.

But before Brussels, we had to travel to Dresden. It was the first ever meeting of the West and East German champions. We'd only won 4-3 at home and Lattek was afraid our dressing-room might be bugged. He also feared they would put something in our food so we took some thermos-flasks with us. We drew 3-3 to go through and had 100,000 fans turn up at our hotel afterwards.

Then we negotiated two more trips to the Eastern bloc. CSKA Sofia and Dosza Ujpest Budapest were relatively straightforward.

In the final in Brussels, I think we had fate on our side. It went to extra-time after a goalless 90 minutes. Luis scored for Atletico with six minutes to go. We were almost dead. But then with only seconds to go, Katsche picked up the ball and took a shot from 25 yards. The ball went in. Katsche didn't score many goals, he was known as 'the Kaiser's cleaner' in defence, but I'm not sure there was a more important goal in the history of the club.

That goal forced a replay that took place two days later. In the second game, we totally overran the Spaniards, who might have been a little demoralised. They did not know what hit them. Hoeness and Müller each scored twice. 4-0. We partied all night long. But the next day, we had to play in Gladbach! At nine in the morning, Lattek had a hard time finding all of us. We managed to sleep a little bit on the coach, but we arrived fairly drunk in Gladbach and lost 5-0. Luckily, we were already champions and the game did not matter.

That year, we were at the peak of our powers. No German club had ever won the European Cup. Bayern were the first. And then half of our team went on to win the World Cup in the summer. German football was never stronger. So it was perhaps inevitable that we would suffer a bit the following season. It was hard to carry on after such a high. Breitner left to play for Real Madrid. We only finished tenth in the league. At one stage it looked as if we could be in a fight against relegation. But when we were playing in Europe, we pulled ourselves together and always raised our level. We stepped up one or two gears.

We made hard work of it in the beginning, as usual. After getting a bye, we were drawn with Magdeburg, the East German champions. They were 2-0 up in Munich at half-time. We came out angry and managed to turn it around and win 3-2. Lattek was worried about food there again, so we took a coach filled like a delicatessen with us. We won 2-1.

Before the quarter-final against Ararat Yerevan of Russia, we lost Lattek as our coach. Dettmar Cramer, known as 'Football Professor', took over. We won 2-0 at home then held out despite losing 1-0 in front of 100,000 fans in Armenia. That was a very exotic location.

Saint-Etienne were a big obstacle in the semi-final. They had humiliated us two years before. But Cramer was very well-prepared. He had everything on them. I think he even knew their shoe sizes. We took a 0-0 draw away from France and won 2-0 at home to reach our second final in a row.

In Paris, Leeds United were considered big favourites at the time. They were very physical. Sadly, Bjorn Andersson's career was finished by a bad tackle from Terry Yorath. His knee was destroyed. Hoeness also got injured. Then their fans lost it after the referee disallowed a Peter Lorimer goal for offside. They ripped out the seats and threw them onto the pitch like frisbees. Bottles were also flying. We feared for our lives. Two policemen were badly injured.

But we kept our cool. 18 minutes from time, Torstensson played a pass to me and I shot with my left foot across goal from outside the box. It crept in at the far post. I was running past all my team-mates towards Cramer to give him a bear-hug. He was a small man. I think I almost suffocated him. I was especially motivated in that game because I was 30 and at the time not certain of getting a new contract. I was a bit angry about it and used that anger to good effect. Later, Müller got a second, in typical fashion.

After the game, we had to stay behind for a long time because there was chaos outside. Fans were throwing stones at the bus which our wives were on, the windows got smashed and cars were burning everywhere. We had a banquet in the hotel and Andersson had to be carried in for it. He was crying. It was a bitter-sweet moment.

Winning the European Cup for a third time in a row became such an important target that our league form really suffered again. We were also popular and had to play friendlies to make money for the club. It was a punishing schedule and almost impossible to play consistently well in the league when you knew that there were European matches ahead.

In the 1975-76 European campaign, we started well for once. We didn't have much trouble with Luxemburg's Jeunesse D'Esch, a little more with Malmö. The Scandinavians were difficult to play. It then became very tricky against Benfica in the Stadium of Light. The country had just seen a dictator deposed. Cramer, however, trusted the hotel cooks. They were a good side and Beckenbauer afterwards complained about losing his hair because he had to make so many defensive headers. We drew 0-0, then were all over them in the second leg which we won 5-1 in the Olympiastadion.

The semi-final against Real Madrid was a real classic. They had Günter Netzer and Breitner, who was injured for the first leg. They took the lead in the Bernabéu. Maier was outstanding, he saved us a few times. Then Müller picked up my pass on the half-way line and just started running. Nobody got near him. It was a wonderful individual goal.

After the final whistle, a young boy ran onto the pitch and hit Müller in the face. He also pushed the linesman to the ground. Hoeness and Müller got involved, so did the Spanish police. In the end, Real were banned from playing at home. Breitner invited us to drink a few beers which he'd had sent over from Bavaria with him. I think he was beginning to feel homesick. In Munich, we played a blinder and won 2-0 thanks to two more goals from Müller. Nobody swapped shirts with Breitner after that game: not because of any bad feelings, but the club wasn't happy if you swapped shirts in those days! The kit-man would get really mad if one or two shirts were missing because then he couldn't use the whole set. It's hard to believe, but true.

So off to Glasgow we went. Hampden Park. Saint-Etienne were our opponents, once again. In a way they had taken over from Ajax as the best attacking side. They had so much flair and we had a lot of respect. We came into that game with a lot of uncertainty. Our fans were also severely out-numbered. The whole of Glasgow was full of green. There was almost no red in the stands. It was like an away match. I don't think we considered ourselves big favourites. On one hand, we had become used to being in a final. On the other, it was really special because we knew we could keep the Cup for good if we won.

As ever, Cramer had all the information we needed and more. He showed us videos of Saint-Etienne's semi-finals. We knew all the players and we knew that they were playing wonderful attacking football. They were pure class.

As I said before, we were already past our peak and knew that all we had were the 'German virtues' of hard work, strong tackling and lots of running. We had no illusions about that. We knew that if we tried outplaying them, they would come out on top. As a footballing side, they were simply too good.

Cramer said, "You have to fight and face up to them." I don't remember much else from his team-talk, to be honest. But he didn't need to say much anyway. It was our chance to write history. We had to take it. No-one in Germany had even come close to three wins in a row before and I'm sure no-one ever will. We didn't talk much, we didn't think about it. As full-blooded footballers, we knew what we had to do in the final. It was the culmination of everything, the highest high. We were 100 per cent concentrated and very tense.

Rummenigge was so nervous that Cramer had to give him two glasses of cognac before the game. There was a lot of pressure on us, for all sorts of reasons. We knew it was the last chance for us to make any waves in Europe. We knew it was realistically our last performance on the big stage. We could not afford to slip up.

The 1970s were a turbulent time. Somebody phoned the stadium, pretending to be the Red Army Faction, the Bader-Meinhof gang, and said they had planted a bomb. The police checked everything out with metal detectors and the game went ahead as planned. We only found out the details afterwards

My job was to mark Jean-Michel Larqué, their captain and playmaker. He was brilliant, a French international, so it was a difficult task. Cramer told me he was my man. "Bulle, if you take him out of the game, that's half the game won," he said. Larqué was the brain of the team. We did not have such a single important player in our side. We were more versatile. Responsibilities were shared. With the French, it was different. They were looking at Larqué for inspiration and guidance, especially in the absence of Rocheteau. He was their main goalscorer and the man we feared most, but he could only start on the bench after getting injured. That was a big help for us.

We had the better start. Müller scored a goal. The referee said it was offside. I'm not so sure. Then Rummenigge, who had calmed down his nerves with alcohol, had a very good shot saved by their goalkeeper Curkovic. Müller tried to pounce on the rebound, but couldn't get there. That was it as far as our chances were concerned.

Saint-Etienne came back into the game strongly. Bathenay hit the bar with a great shot and Maier saved the follow-up header from Revelli. They put a lot of pressure on us. Santini even hit the bar again with a header before half-time. We were quite lucky to go in at 0-0, but we still fancied our chances at this stage. Maier went up to the referee and complained about the ball. He said, "Hey Mister, ball too soft. Must pump air and make harder!" I'm not sure the ball was any harder in the second half.

We managed to contain them after the break. Then Müller was fouled outside their box in the 57th minute. It was about 22 metres out, almost central, slightly to the left. That was my sort of distance. I had the hardest shot and I also had the accuracy. It had been the plan that I should take the free-kicks. They had six men in their wall.

Beckenbauer was standing over the ball and we were thinking about the options. Lifting it over the wall would have been difficult. Curkovic was a great keeper, and it was hard to curl it and get the necessary power at the same time. So we decided to have a go.

Franz said, "I will pass it across to the right of the wall."

I said, "You have to get it right, Franz."

So he rolled it across and I hit it. The ball passed the wall and bulged the net just inside the post. Curkovic had no chance. By the time he threw himself across the goal, it had already gone in. You couldn't have imagined it could be more perfect. There were so many factors: it could have hit the wall, or gone for a corner. But everything went right on that occasion. It was the perfect strike, no dispute! We needed a fair amount of luck for that, but it came off.

It was a wonderful feeling to score, but the game was not finished. There was plenty of time to play yet. We were really pushed. It was hard work. I don't remember thinking, "Okay, we've done it now."

1-0 is not very comfortable, especially in a final. The last 30 minutes just wouldn't pass. Time almost stood still, the minutes passed so slowly. It took an eternity. We were hell-bent on defending our lead. Hoeness and me had some chances on the break, but the pressure from the French was nearly unbearable. They did everything to get the equaliser. But we denied them. Maier was outstanding. And we were fighting until the death. It was one big fight, pure rear-guard action. We were trembling right until the very end.

The phrase, 'it's not over until the final whistle' is a cliché, but it's also the truth. Every footballer knows you cannot afford to relax for one second. Luck, discipline and raw passion saw us through in the end. It wasn't an undeserved victory, but it was a fortunate one. Saint-Etienne had been better on the night, I think. We defended our title, that's all we could do. We defended it, tooth and nail. Our style had become much more defensive and tactical in comparison to the late 1960s. We did not have the same fluidity. But we had the experience to hold out and make the most of our chances. The cautious football under Cramer became Bayern's trademark and lasted throughout the 1980s even though different managers had different ideas.

When the final whistle came, it was ecstasy. Euphoria. A kind of rush took hold of me. I was running and screaming and hugging everybody around me, half of whom were strangers, but I didn't care at all. After a while, I looked for Larqué to console him and swap shirts - I took a risk this time! We had fought a running battle and at times it had been quite hairy, but we shook hands and everything was forgotten. That's the way it should be. I still have his shirt at home.

A few minutes later, I was lifting the European Cup for the third time amidst hundreds of fans. That feeling is impossible to describe. Of all the happy moments at Bayern, that was my happiest. It was the absolute highlight of my career. A wonderful, wonderful evening. All the tension had given way to relief. Slowly, we started realising the magnitude of what we had achieved. We were too tired to have a long party in the dressing-room. The game had been too hard for us.

In the hotel, there was the usual banquet with speeches from Cramer and our President Neudecker. It was nice, but we were so knackered that we didn't get to celebrate much afterwards. There was no great atmosphere at the dinner, there was no comparison to Brussels.

Winning had become a little bit routine. It was a lovely evening and a dream come true, but everybody seemed a bit lost in their own thoughts. I knew my career was coming to a close and we knew that Beckenbauer would leave to play with Pelé in New York. Maier was getting on a bit. Maybe we had one or two years to go, but this team had essentially run its course. We knew it and Neudecker knew it; even though he said he wished we could stay together for longer. A new generation would take over soon. The triumph was definitely tinged with sadness. Something was missing after all these years. We had been 19 and 20-year old boys when we had won our first trophies and six or seven of us had never left the club. Maybe we had seen a little too much

Captains Robert Jonquet and Miguel Muñoz exchange banners
before the first ever European Cup Final

My header bounces into the net to put Reims 3-2 ahead, but Madrid
managed to score twice to win the trophy

My great friend and room-mate 'Pancho' Puskas scores his hat-trick goal
in one of the best finals of all time

We salute the Hampden Park crowd after our fifth final win. Far left is
Alfredo di Stéfano, the greatest player of all time, while I am next to
goalkeeper Rogelio Dominguez

I never thought we would lose even though we went behind to an early goal from Sándor Kocsis (second left), but it was unnecessary to concede

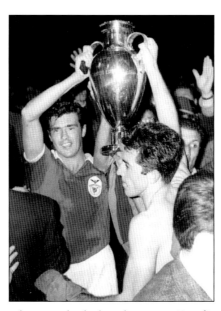

An incredible feeling, but no alcohol at the party! Benfica captain Jose Aguas (left) is the first non-Real Madrid player to hold aloft the European Cup

We had five attackers against Real but needed heroes at the back like
Aristide Guarneri (centre) to keep out Ferenc Puskas (left)

Rafael Felo's shot beats our goalkeeper Giuliano Sarti (left) but we were
leading 3-0 at the time and I was waiting for the final whistle

Tommy Gemmell (second from right) turns away after equalising for us.
He scored in the 1970 final as well, an incredible achievement

My one regret: it was a team success but I picked up the Cup on my own.
Even now I wish we had all been there

We had an undoubted advantage at Wembley because most of the neutrals there were supporting us

I won't let go of this one, lads! On the lap of honour, I am far left holding the trophy with Bobby Charlton while Tony Dunne offers his support

Just four minutes gone and my header flew past Dino Zoff to put us one goal ahead. Here I celebrate with Ruud Krol

Johan Cruyff and Barry Hulshoff parade the trophy around the Belgrade Stadium

My team-mates (in white) wheel away in delight to celebrate my curling effort past the Saint-Etienne goalkeeper. I couldn't have hit it any better

I screamed and hugged everyone after the final whistle, but lifting the European Cup for the third time was the absolute highlight of my career
It was ecstasy!

If I had thought about the amount of people that wanted me to score that
penalty, I might have missed.
But despite changing my mind about where to put it, I scored!

Jimmy Case (left) and I get to know our first European Cup. I won
another three, but the first is always the best

Hamburg goalkeeper Rudi Kargus can only watch as John Robertson's shot goes past him for the winner, which sealed our second straight European Cup

I'm not giving this medal to anyone! I sit in front of the team, remembering that a year earlier, manager Brian Clough (far left) wanted all our medals

Football is meant to be fun and joy but that night was a dark, horrible nightmare. I still pray for the families of the victims every night

Michel Platini scores the winning penalty. Michel wanted to give everything up after the game. In his head was the fact that a Frenchman had come to see him play and died

Ruud Gullit scores his second to make it 3-0 before half-time.
If there is such a thing as a perfect game, this was it

The team celebrates with Silvio Berlusconi (second row, suited),
who had been our inspiration for exciting football.
I am behind him and next to Marco van Basten

The moment that changed French football history: I beat Frank Rijkaard to head home the winning goal. I have not bought a drink in Marseille since!

Eric de Meco (with the trophy on his head) leads the celebrations and is helped by (from left) Franck Sauzee, Bernard Tapie, myself and Didier Deschamps

It happened so fast: Teddy Sheringham (above) equalised and then Ole Gunnar Solskjaer scored the winner. I was proud yet still felt I hadn't contributed

When we travelled through Manchester on the bus, and saw all the people celebrating, I knew I had been a part of history

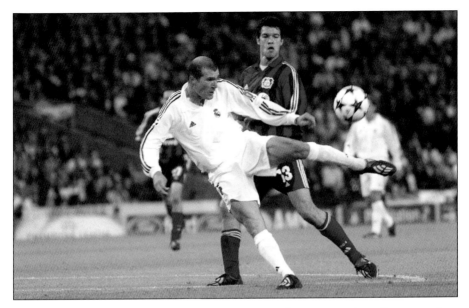

The moment people remember: Zinedine Zidane's superb volley was the winning goal. It was our third success in five years, so we marked an era

I kept out this shot from Dimitar Berbatov (right) with my feet but they kept coming at us. When you make a save you think,
"Hey, this lot could score! This is dangerous!" Notice the badly-cut sleeves

Six minutes of madness: Xabi Alonso has his penalty saved but fires in the rebound to make it 3-3. We're back in the game!

The local boys done good: Stevie G and I hold aloft the European Cup while penalty hero Djibril Cissé looks on

of each other. Off the pitch, the harmony was gone, we hardly hung out together like we used to.

Everybody had their families, I had a son, and the priorities had changed. And we were definitely not getting better. Our powers were waning. We knew it would not last. Just like Ajax before us, we had come to the end of the cycle. It was inevitable. I think Neudecker even warned us of the dangers of winning too much at the banquet. Where can you go from there as a footballer? You can only go down.

I later heard that Saint-Etienne were welcomed like heroes in Paris by the French president Giscard D'Estaing and driven along the Champs-Elysees. In Munich, there was almost nothing. No after-party.

Everybody went their separate ways. Everybody just went home. For many years, thousands of fans had welcomed us on the Marienplatz. There were always big public parties, but in 1976 it was very low-key. There was no big celebration. Everybody had got used to our success. Glasgow was the last big adventure of a wonderful team.

Fortunately, we have managed to stay in touch. We meet regularly at golf tourn-aments, and Rummenigge is the only one who does not play. It's funny because we only started playing golf before the 1976 final in Scotland. Naturally, we have a laugh and wind each other up and talk about the good old days. There is never a lack of material and it's always very funny, especially with Maier around. I'm just thankful I was able to be part of it and help Bayern win all those trophies.

PHIL NEAL
DEFENDER 1975–1985

BORN 29th February 1951, Irchester, Northamptonshire
SIGNED from Northampton Town, October 1974; £66,000
LIVERPOOL CAREER 648 games, 60 goals
HONOURS 8 English League titles, 4 European Cups, 1 UEFA Cup,
4 League Cups, 50 England caps
LEFT Free transfer to Bolton, December 1985 to become player-manager

When it comes to a medal haul, it is impossible to beat Phil Neal. Neal won
more medals and collected more honours than any other Red, including four
of Liverpool's five European Cups. His consistency along with a huge will to
win made him a stalwart in sides managed by Bob Paisley, Joe Fagan and briefly
Kenny Dalglish. The latter summed up his quiet ability when he called him
"the best player I ever played with".

Liverpool 3 v Borussia Mönchengladbach 1

Wednesday 25 May 1977

Olympic Stadium, Rome
Attendance 52,078

Liverpool win the first of their five European Cups

Teams

Ray Clemence	1	Wolfgang Kneib
Phil Neal	2	Bertie Vogts
Joey Jones	3	Hans Klinkhammer
Tommy Smith	4	Hans-Jürgen Wittkamp
Ray Kennedy	5	Rainer Bonhof
Emlyn Hughes	6	Horst Wohlers
		(sub. Wilfred Hannes)
Kevin Keegan	7	Allan Simonsen
Jimmy Case	8	Herbert Wimmer
		(sub. Christian Kulik)
Steve Heighway	9	Uli Stielike
Terry McDermott	10	Frank Schaffer
Ian Callaghan	11	Jupp Heynckes
McDermott 27, Smith 64, Neal (pen) 82	**Scorers**	Simonsen 51

Referee: Wurtz (France)

THERE WE ALL are, sitting at breakfast, none of us having had any sleep. It's the morning after the night before and us players are on top of the world, well Europe, but you know what I mean. The jokes and the singing haven't stopped and then there's Bob, making his way into the dining room. As usual he had on his old cardigan, full of holes, his old slippers on his feet and his tabloid newspaper rolled up in his back pocket. This morning though, there was something different. Something extra. In his arms was the European Cup and he wasn't going to let it go. I'll never forget that sight. We all just looked and marvelled at the man who had made us European Champions; we just stood and let out a huge cheer.

It was, to coin a phrase, the best of times. To go to a city like Rome and win the European Cup for the first time in the manner that we did was magical. The team, the fans, the match, everything was perfect and it's a night that everyone involved will always cherish. I know I will. We'd had an amazing season and hoped to win all three trophies still up for grabs at the end of it. That wasn't to be as we lost the FA Cup final after winning the League, but with Bob Paisley at the helm, we were determined to make Liverpool football club the Kings of Europe.

It had been a tough start, though, for both us players and for Bob himself, who'd struggled to live up to the legend that was Bill Shankly. Just after I signed I watched the lads get knocked out of the Cup Winners' Cup by the Hungarian side Ferencvaros and things were clearly a struggle. Bob admitted to the lads in that Durham accent of his that he "didn't want the bloody job anyway".

Things weren't running smoothly. Bob was finding his feet and, of course, what didn't help was that Shanks would be turning up at Melwood, making his presence felt and confusing all those players who had played under him. To them he was 'The Boss', but to Bob, Joe and Ronnie it was like having Bill on the bench with them and something had to be done. He had to be shunned by some of the men who had worked with him so closely for so many years. Those same men now had to get on with building for more success, constructing Bob's team.

That's where I came in. I was Bob's first signing. I'd been playing since the age of sixteen for Northampton and had over 230 games under my belt. I'd caught the eye with plenty of goals from midfield where I played at the time. Part of me felt that my time may have passed and at 23 maybe I wasn't going to get a move to a big club; I was wrong.

Newspapers used to rant on about this goalscoring midfield player from Northampton, but I wasn't sure if any of the big clubs were paying much attention. Bob Paisley was. He sent Geoff Twentyman, his chief scout, down to the Cobblers. Geoff had an incredible record when it came to spotting talent and was responsible for a conveyor belt of brilliant players making their way to Anfield. Kevin Keegan, Ray Clemence, myself, and later there was Ian Rush. He was great at that. But when he came along to see me I ended up playing two-thirds of the match in goal. Liverpool were planning to spend £66,000 on me and there I am standing between the sticks. We won the game, mind, and I kept a clean sheet, so perhaps that proved my versatility. Anyway, Geoff must have liked what he saw.

At the press conference to announce my signing, Bob said that he hadn't seen me play, but he knew I could play in every position across the back four and was naturally two-footed. That would do him and that gave me great heart. I realised that ability might just win me my chance.

My opportunity came along quicker than I imagined. I had only played four reserve games when I got my first break and what a game to start with. It was a Saturday morning and I was all prepared to play for the reserves, whilst the first team had a derby match at Goodison. Tom Saunders, Bob's advisor, came round to my digs that morning and said there was a problem with one of the full-backs so Bob wanted me to join the first team squad.

I was a little nervous, but I thought, "Part of the squad, OK, that's fine." We went to Anfield to pick up my boots and I asked if we would be taking the car and Tom says, "No, we'll walk across the park." So there I am walking to Goodison with my boots in a brown paper bag amid thousands of Scousers all asking me for tickets. This is my first experience of the Merseyside derby, remember, and I couldn't believe how electric the atmosphere was.

I was just enjoying taking in the whole day, enjoying the occasion, but then I walk into the dressing-room. "Get ready, son," says Bob. "You're playing." "Bloody hell." I never had a chance to phone my Mum or anything. I went out in front of the crowd and I thought, "If I can cope with this then I can cope with anything that life throws at me," and I did. That day was my base.

We drew 0-0 and I jumped for joy, cuddling Emlyn Hughes like we'd won the League. There's 56,000 fans thinking, "Who the heck is this fella?"! It was a great start for me and was an early hint at the genius of Bob Paisley. Bob hadn't allowed me to dwell on the fact that I would be playing in a Merseyside derby and so told me at the last minute. He was so clever was Bob.

I appreciated that I was around some great players and I had to learn to have confidence, not arrogance. I played at left-back as I had for the first 18 months of my career and got on with it. That derby game gave me a bucketful of confidence and, although I went back into the reserves for a couple of matches, I managed to break back into the first team and then didn't miss a League match for nine years or so. Life didn't get much better than playing for Liverpool Football Club. Ray Kennedy was coming through, Terry McDermott too and soon local boys Jimmy Case and David Fairclough would arrive as Bob's team started to take shape.

That first season of Bob being in charge finished without any silverware. We ended up as runners-up to Derby in the League, but I was soon taught that isn't good enough for Liverpool. I was quite excited by being a runner-up in the English First Division and looked forward to picking up some sort of medal. "Oh no, you don't get them, son." Don't be ridiculous. Liverpool did not celebrate finishing second. You don't get congratulated for falling below the highest standard. What you do get is inspired to win it the following year.

I was learning so much. I trained hard and kept my head down. I was lucky to be next to Ian Callaghan in the dressing-room, who was a brilliant example. Get in early, cup of tea, don't be rushed, train well, play well. I learnt all that from Cally, which was great, but generally I kept myself to myself, to start with that is.

The following season, 1975-76, was vital, but is mostly forgotten because of what subsequent teams went on to achieve. We won both the League title and the UEFA Cup with a side that had quickly become very hard to beat. We had to win our last game at Wolves and were struggling at 0-1 down, but managed three goals in the last fifteen minutes and the fans went ballistic. I think that night in the Midlands was the start; that was the moment the fans and players knew we were back. Bob began to act like the manager. Bill's ghost had been laid to rest.

That meant we were in the European Cup for 1976-77 and we were desperate to go one better and win the biggest prize of all. We were a confident bunch, but had to endure a strange pre-season with all the talk about whether Kevin Keegan would be staying or going. That continued on for the entire campaign, with what felt like daily paper-talk about Kevin's destination abroad. We knew he was off, but the whole thing could be a little distracting. Kevin became the butt of a few jokes and Smithy wouldn't let up, calling him "Concessions Keegan".

We'd all arrive for training at Melwood on a Monday morning, but no Kevin. "What supermarket is he opening this morning, Bob?" Smithy would ask. "What formation next week, Bob, 4-4-1?" Tommy was senior enough to get away with that. He was a man of the city and it upset him that sometimes Kevin was out busy doing other things. I admire Liverpudlians for that. They are bold enough to say it how it is and that's what Tommy did.

We were told that Kevin wanted new challenges in Europe, but we all knew that deep down he wanted to double his wages. No-one minded that, but I would have liked him to just come out and say it. When Souness left in 1984 he called us all together and said, "Lads, I am going for the money. See you later."

It was light-hearted with Kevin though and the team got on with playing well and winning honours. By Christmas, when we knew that Keegan was definitely off, we were challenging for everything and actually wanted to give him a good send-off. The European Cup was well under way and we were looking good.

We started out playing Crusaders, the champions of Northern Ireland. We beat them 2-0 at Anfield and they were ecstatic at that result. It seemed the whole of Northern Ireland came out to see us in the second leg and thousands were scaling lampposts, drainpipes and trees to try and get a glimpse of us. We were in the dressing-room and there were loads of people trying to get in and have us sign autographs. This is before the game, remember, and Bob's face was a picture.

"Get them bloody out of here, Joe! Get them out." He was worried that this game wasn't finished yet and didn't want us feeling as if we were playing a friendly. As it was, we went out there focused and won the game 5-0. Next was Trabzonspor in Turkey. I missed the first leg through an injury. Everton's centre-forward Bob Latchford had given me a dead leg in the derby game the week before and it sounded like the big man did me a huge favour. Thanks, Bob.

Tom Saunders had come back from his scouting mission saying it was bit dodgy out there, but the lads returned, having lost 1-0, effing and blinding about what a terrible place it was. The worst they'd ever seen. They were well pleased with having only lost by the one goal, that's how bad the trip had been. I played in the second leg and we won 3-0.

So, we went into 1977 looking forward to a quarter-final against Saint-Etienne. They were a class outfit, they really were. The tie has gone down in Liverpool folklore. We lost out there 1-0, but the game at Anfield will never be forgotten. The intensity of that night has only been matched by the recent game against Chelsea, both were so similar and both were testimony to what football means to Liverpool's supporters. We scored early through Kevin, but Bathenay got a vital away goal for the Frenchmen before half-time. Ray Kennedy then put us ahead on the night, but we still needed to score again to go through.

The game is rightly remembered for David Fairclough's goal. What a player David was. People have gone on about Solskjaer, but Fairclough was the original "Supersub". I played 450-odd consecutive league games and I don't think David got 450 minutes, yet he'll always be remembered because of that night.

Saint-Etienne had some great players such as striker Dominique Rocheteau and what has been forgotten about that night is that we still had about eight minutes to play once David had netted his fantastic strike to make it 3-2 on aggregate. For those eight minutes, the French battered us and we were hanging on. Fingernail stuff. We were kicking them off the line, there were critical tackles, Clem last-ditch saves, the lot. It was incredible. That was the only game that my concentration went from the field of play to the stands. The noise, the movement; people didn't want to sit down and were twitching about they were so nervous. If we had not won that night we might never have seen the great river of success that followed.

The semi-final was a bit of an anti-climax, but we had to be wary because the Swiss team FC Zurich weren't bad. We noticed that they could be pulled about a bit at free-kicks, so we worked hard on that in training. They were so rigid in their marking that you could be clever and that's what we were. Jimmy Case and I worked on a free-kick and it came off out there early on and I got in to score. We won 3-1 in the first-leg with me getting a second thanks to a penalty and on the journey home the boys were planning for the European Cup final.

That, though, simply wasn't allowed. We had to bite our tongues, as the management weren't ever going to allow any complacency. We kept our heads and won comfortably 3-0; 6-1 on aggregate. So we were off to Rome. It was a mad few weeks. We won the Championship again and got to the FA Cup final, so there were a lot of meetings, suits to be fitted, tickets to be allocated and songs to be recorded.

It was down to Wembley first for the FA Cup final in which we got beat. It was strange. Not a lot went wrong that day apart from the fact that we lost 2-1. Tommy Docherty actually said his Manchester United side had played shit and still won that game. We may have won it if Bob had picked the eleven that would play in and win the European Cup, but we had so much belief in ourselves and such a great team spirit that we just had to get on with things.

Bob built his team around people who could captain the club. Clem, Smithy, Thompson, Kevin, myself, Emlyn, later Souey. That was Bob's idea, he knew that the more players who were mentally strong and who were natural leaders the better for the team, and that night, after losing the FA Cup, we all had to be strong.

So there we were at Harrow station, a group of players who had just been beaten by their arch rivals at Wembley in a showpiece final. We should have been gutted, but it was Clem – who had been so disappointed by his own display – who suddenly said, "Fuck it, let's get pissed," and starts dancing there and then on the platform. That was that. The journey home turned into a party with the wives and us players enjoying a drink and a giggle. We had Jimmy Tarbuck on board, who set the tone and, after some drinks, some laughs and some bonding, the United slip-up was out of our minds. We had the European Cup final against Borussia Mönchengladbach of Germany to think about in a matter of days. Onwards and upwards.

Having slept it off on the Sunday we trained hard on the Monday at Melwood before boarding our Aer Lingus flight to Rome on the Tuesday, all decked out in our dapper new suits and ready to go to work. The wives and girlfriends flew out separately and enjoyed a day and a night out in Rome whilst we went to our hotel, had a light training season and got our heads down for a good night's sleep.

I roomed with Clem and I woke him for breakfast at 9am. I was always waiting on Clem. I used to tell him he could play until he was 40. He never had to move on the pitch and I was doing everything for him off of it.

We had a light stretch and then returned to the hotel for a lunch of chicken or steak, fish and some beans. For some reason there was always plenty of toast. No bread, no rolls allowed, just stacks of toast. You could have 300,000 pieces of toast, but no bread. I never did work that out.

It was 1pm and time for the team meeting. If the lunch had been our usual menu, Bob's meeting certainly wasn't. Bob never did go on too much about the opposition, but that afternoon he didn't mention them at all. He sat us down and started going on about the war. "The last time I was in Rome, I was in a tank liberating the place," he said. "I took on the Germans back then and you'll do it tonight." We were in hysterics, but a part of me wanted to know about the Dane, Allan Simonsen, who I would be marking. He was European Player of the Year that season and a dangerous player. How should I play him? Who knows. Instead Bob was telling us how hard he had worked in the war to give us youngsters a better world and now was the time to repay him.

Bob knew what he was doing, though. Right at the end he went on to reveal how we would be playing and it would transpire that Bob's tactics were spot on. Mönchengladbach had been destroyed in the 1973 UEFA Cup final by John Toshack and feared his ability in the air. Bob knew Tosh would miss this game through injury, but kept him in the squad just to keep them on their toes. Kevin would be on his own up front, pulling the defenders all over the place, whilst Stevie Heighway would work off of him.

As for telling us about the opposition's strengths and weaknesses, Bob wasn't one to dwell, and anyway he could never remember people's names. He would use the word, "Do-ins" when he couldn't recall individuals. We never knew why he used that word, he just did. It was "Watch Do-ins out on the left, he's tricky," or "Get at Do-ins at right-back, he's had a knee injury." He had so many quirks, Bob. He once said to me, "Phil, watch the winger, he's not quick, but he's nippy." He'd say this team tend to "Ponk" it. "What's Ponk?" Smithy would ask! He never did get a straight answer. That was Bob. Somehow he got his point across.

Having had our 'chat' we went to our rooms for an afternoon nap. I loved those and had no problem, however big the game, dropping off. Clem and I slept and then it was downstairs for some tea and of course some more toast, and then it was onto the bus and off to the Olympic stadium for the European Cup final.

We arrived at the beautiful stadium and went out to check the pitch. It was then that it hit us just how many fans had made the trip. We knew they had spent money on the journey to Wembley and had heard that they had sold fridges and cars, or anything to raise the money to make it out to Rome. It hit us when we walked out and saw that incredible sea of red and white and more flags than I've ever seen. Stevie Heighway came over to me. "Phil," he said. "Look at that, mate. We have to win for them. We have to win tonight for all those people out there."

I remember the pitch was very hard, but luckily the studs I'd worn all season were quite worn and perfect for the surface. Soon though, you're in the dressing-room and it's time to get out there and make history. We walked out (it's a bloody long walk at Rome's Olympic Stadium) alongside the Germans and all I could think was how tall their keeper, Wolfgang Kneib was. Look at the size of him! He was about three inches bigger than Clem, who wasn't small. He's towering over us all and I remember thinking then, "If I get a penalty, I'll have to keep it low."

As we stood there waiting for the whistle you could tell that all that disappointment from the weekend, all that depression was gone. We were ready.

Early on everyone was getting good confidence-building touches and it became clear that Kevin was going to give the great Bertie Vogts a torrid night. He pulled him all over the place and Vogts began to get annoyed, tripping Kevin up left, right and centre. I myself felt good early on after I managed an important block from a Heynckes shot. From then on I was always wanting the ball. Whenever Clem had it he always looked to bowl it out to me.

That was an unsaid thing. Clem picks up the ball, I peeled to the touchline to receive it and start something off. That night I had Cally always showing inside saying, "If I'm tightly marked, don't worry. Give it to me and I'll give it back. Let's move them about a bit." It was a European style of football. We could dictate the pace of a game and that's exactly what we started to do.

I was enjoying it. "Come on, Jimmy," I said to Case, who was ahead of me on the right flank. "You and me, let's make this Simonsen worry about us." We had a lot of the ball and I was enjoying getting forward. It was great having Jimmy there. He didn't mind doing all the grafting in front of me and that would leave a lot of room for me to get past him and into the opposition's half.

We had to be careful, though. Just after the half hour, Rainer Bonhof, a great player, strode into our half and unleashed a shot, that to be fair, beat Clem. But it struck the upright. It was the only sniff the Germans had in that first period, whilst we were looking dangerous each time we got near their penalty box.

Ray Kennedy brought a good save from Kneib, while a Case shot was cleared. We were happy with how it was going, but, just before half-time, it got better. It was a tactical night. It was in many ways Bob's win and the goal that put us ahead was perfect as it was exactly how Bob had hoped we would open them up.

Kevin had been told to be 'The Lone Star' up front, taking Vogts away from the central area and out onto the flanks and his decoy run was ideal. Stevie Heighway drifted in with the ball, saw Terry Mac's run from deep and slipped it through, Terry received the pass and bang, goal. It was absolutely perfect and showed what a master tactician Bob was.

We were on top, but during the break we were told to be wary. "Hang on," the management said. "They're going to have a go at us and we have to be on our guard." Unfortunately, it wasn't long before we were forced to listen as it took Mönchengladbach only minutes of the second half to draw level.

It was a mix up between Jimmy and myself. He thought I was further back than I was. I'd started to go on ahead of him and Jimmy passed it straight to Simonsen, who battered the ball into the top corner. I was right behind it and I knew it was in straight away. It was a huge blow, but I had to make sure Jimmy's head didn't drop. He needed cajoling as he was down about the goal. He was very quiet and had gone within himself. They were mounting attacks down our side and so I'm saying, "Come on Jimmy, it's gone. Let's get back on this."

From then they really put us under pressure. Clem made some fine saves, one brilliant block from Stielike and I recall thinking, "Bloody hell, I'm glad he's here tonight." People forget we were under the cosh for a good while and Clem saved us twice with world-class goalkeeping. Up front Kevin and Stevie weren't getting many openings. They ran tirelessly, but could they hurt the Germans, whose real Achilles heel was in the air? I'd forgive anyone for thinking the answer to that was "No". It was going to be up to one of the rest of us to pull something out of the bag; but who? We'd all been pegged back as the Germans pushed forward.

Having soaked up a lot of pressure, we won a corner. I was glad of the rest and Smithy, who never went up for corners, said, "Cover me, Phil, I fancy this."

"Alright, Smithy, no problem. Up you go."

Bob always afforded us that freedom. There were no rigid rules about who went where at set-pieces and if you fancied it, up you went. So off went Smithy.

Who would have thought it? In what was supposed to be his last game (he eventually went on for another season at Anfield), Smithy connected with as good a header as you'll ever see and we're 2-1 up. Brilliant! It was his testimonial on the following Friday, so he obviously felt if he scored the winning goal he might get a few more fans in and line his pockets a bit. Typical Smithy!

We might have been leading again, but the Germans weren't going to stop getting at us and they soon had us under the cosh. To help, Kevin dropped back into our half and he picked up the ball deep and he went on this diagonal run at Bertie Vogts. It took the ball and the pressure as far down the field as possible and was just what we needed. What a clever run, Kevin. He just went and went and went, with Vogts nipping way at his heels. Eventually Vogts was forced to make a challenge that the ref saw as a foul. Penalty!

Fantastic! You'd have thought so wouldn't you? The ref points to the spot and my first reaction is, "Oh Christ, it's all on me now!" I'm fifty yards away and I have to make what felt like a hell of a long walk to the penalty box. There's eight minutes left and if I score, it's all over. If I miss...

Emlyn looks at me with desperation in his eyes, Smithy looks at me with one of those, "Score this or I'm breaking your fucking back," stares and Cally, who had never been booked and is so quiet and polite, shouts, "Hey, Nealy, stick this in will ya."

I was very confident when it came to penalties. I had done a book with Clem on the art of taking and saving penalties, so I ought to have known what to do. One of the rules was vital – don't change your mind. I looked at the keeper, picked the ball up and thought, "Come on, this is my turn." Then, "Keeper's left, keeper's left," I'm telling myself as I put the ball down. But, as I turn and run-up I've changed my mind. Blind panic. I did the same in the FA Cup against Brighton in 1983 and missed, but this time God is on my side. The keeper goes the other way and the ball's in the net.

It wasn't until I got home and saw the photos that I noticed as I was running up to take it Cally, who had played 800 odd games, is praying; literally standing on the edge of the area praying for me to score. Bloody hell, there was a lot on my shoulders. That goal meant a lot. If I had thought about the numbers of people that wanted me to score that penalty, the amount of fans whose lives almost depend on your success, I probably would have missed.

The bench were going crazy. Fairclough, Tommo, Tosh, Alan Waddle. They were all so happy. I was so elated and so relieved. Wolfgang Kneib, I will always remember his name, his height and his eyes as I went on that run-up.

After that the legs felt good. We were all full of running. Terry McDermott, especially, was covering acres. He could go all day, even after ten pints of lager. He was a great athlete. Tommy Smith was coming to an end and his will to win urged us on. Cally had been there since the start and his quiet but professional attitude was so vital to all of us. Whilst Kevin was off to Hamburg and we wanted to give him something to say, "Bye". Joey Jones was so passionate, so hyper and such a lift in the dressing-room. He had been a fan and it showed.

We all wanted it so much. We had proven our worth. Mentally we had been so strong. We were so gutted to lose that FA Cup, but now we had won the biggest prize of all. The whistle blew and it was just sheer joy. I went straight to Clem and hugged him. "What a year, mate."

So, it was time to celebrate. We had put so much in both physically and mentally that season and now was the time to let our perms down and party. The press were there, the fans got into the Holiday Inn and it was mayhem to be fair. The food went like locusts had got to it, but it didn't matter. You never fancy any food after a match anyway. We didn't mind, we wanted to share it with whomever. A load of Scousers at a free party. You can imagine, can't you? The food went, the ale went, it was magic. At about two o'clock we all went to Stevie Heighway's room and carried on there.

By morning we were all around the pool and, footballers being footballers, people were soon being thrown in. I had bought some new shoes from Russell and Bromley for about £80, which was quite a few quid back in 1977, and Kevin is trying to get me in. "I've got a shitty watch on that I don't care about that, but let me get my Russell and Bromleys off," I cried. Kevin was having none of it and in the play-struggle I caught him under the eye with my thumb. Kevin came home with a real shiner and the press were adamant that Smithy had hit him, but it wasn't that at all, it was me trying to protect my new shoes.

It's really when you return that you realise how many people you've touched. Thousands of fans are there to say, "Thank you" and that is special. We wanted to say, "Thanks" to them because their role in our success was vital. Ask today's players, they'll tell you. Liverpool got through tough games against the likes of Juventus and Chelsea to win the 2005 Champions League because of the fans and the desire they transmit from the stands down onto the pitch.

It was a wonderful summer. One I'll never forget. It was the Queen's Jubilee year, Virginia Wade won Wimbledon and then there was Bob. A simple man, but a brilliant one. I can't believe he didn't get a knighthood. It was such a privilege to be around him. I never missed a day's training because I loved it so much. Heavy cold? I'm in. Slight knock? I'm in. I didn't want to give them an excuse to rest me and I didn't want to miss a day with the players and the staff.

It was such a fun place to be. There was so much laughter, so much joking about but, my God, once we crossed that line, there was nothing but a dogged determination to win. Wherever we went, be it Poland or the Nou Camp there was always a belief and a drive to be the best.

It was like Bob had built a Roman Army and sent us out to conquer Europe.

KENNY BURNS
DEFENDER 1977–1981

BORN   23rd September 1953, Glasgow, Scotland
SIGNED   1977 from Birmingham City; £150,000
NOTTINGHAM FOREST CAREER   137 games, 13 goals
HONOUR   2 English League titles, 2 English League Cups,
2 European Cups, 20 Scotland caps
LEFT   Transferred to Leeds, 1981; £400,000

Kenny Burns was a striker with a reputation for bad behaviour when Forest
assistant coach Peter Taylor persuaded Brian Clough to sign him. Despite having
played for Scotland as a forward, Burns spent his Forest career at centre-back
alongside Larry Lloyd, and won Football Writers' Footballer of the Year in his
first season. He was a mainstay of Forest's European Cup-winning sides and
was a cult hero among fans for his powerful tackles and never-say-die attitude.
He spent three years at Leeds before becoming player-manager at non-league
Telford. Since then, he has worked for Forest's corporate department and now
hosts a regular radio-show on Century FM.

Nottingham Forest 1 v SV Hamburg 0

Wednesday 28 May 1980

Santiago Bernabéu Stadium, Madrid
Attendance 51,000

Nottingham Forest, the side from the smallest city ever to win the European Cup,
become the second English team to successfully defend their European title

Teams

Peter Shilton	1	Rudi Kargus
Viv Anderson	2	Manny Kaltz
Frank Gray	3	Peter Nogly
(sub. Bryn Gunn)		
Larry Lloyd	4	Ivan Buljan
Kenny Burns	5	Ditmar Jakobs
Martin O'Neill	6	Holger Hieronymus
		(sub. Horst Hrubesch)
John McGovern	7	Felix Magath
Ian Bowyer	8	Caspar Memering
Gary Mills	9	Kevin Keegan
(sub. John O'Hare)		
John Robertson	10	Willi Reimann
Gary Birtles	11	Jürgen Milewski

Robertson 21	**Scorers**	

Referee: Garrido (Portugal)

The tunnel at the Santiago Bernabéu stadium was magnificent. It was practically the length of the pitch going back inside the stadium and on either side, there were ten-foot high glass cabinets filled with trophies. It was quite a sight. This is where we stood before the game, waiting for our second European Cup final in as many years.

We were up against Hamburg, the favourites. Hamburg had beaten mighty Real Madrid 5-1 in the semi-final and boasted Kevin Keegan, a double European Footballer of the Year, in their side. My central defensive partner Larry Lloyd went up to Kevin in that tunnel, right up to him, and he said, "Kevin, Kenny's not in a good mood tonight." He just wanted to plant a seed of doubt in his mind.

Keegan knew that if one of us had the chance to get stuck into him early on, we would. I remember after ten minutes, that chance came. It was a 50-50 tackle on the touchline and we both went in for it. It was a hard, honest tackle, but I just edged it. As the game went on, Keegan started dropping back into midfield to get the ball, then he went alongside his full-backs and he was even receiving passes from his own goalkeeper. Well, he was good, but he couldn't score from his own box. We were determined to win our individual battles as whoever won the battles won the match. I felt like I won the battle against him that night. I went in to the game knowing I was playing against Kevin Keegan, but by the end of the game, he knew he had been up against Kenny Burns.

The funny thing was, I had been a striker at my previous club Birmingham and had scored 20 goals in the old First Division for them. Brian Clough was the Nottingham Forest manager and when his assistant, Peter Taylor, suggested they buy me, he said, "What do we want with that trouble-maker?" I had been bombed out by Birmingham after a few incidents, but Taylor had followed me to the dog-tracks to make sure I was behaving.

I met with Clough on a Sunday. We went to Gregory's Rose Garden together. They were doing a sweet pea show that day. I thought I might get some mushy peas out of it, but it was a flower show. No food.

I went with my wife and Peter drove us round the area, showed us some houses, then we went to the club and signed the contract. We had some champagne then Clough said, "Right, get your hair cut and I'll see you Monday." I didn't see him for over a week after that.

We had ten days of pre-season and Clough had gone on holiday. He left us with Jimmy Gordon, the coach. At that time of year, we just did running and got ourselves fit. It was all about how quickly you could recover. Peter Withe was there, and he could run forever. When he left, Garry Birtles came and did the same. Jimmy mainly took us running. That was our training. We never practiced free-kicks or corners. But we did have practice games. On the Friday the first team was due to take on the reserves. He stood up and said, "You lot, put on these bibs: Middleton, Anderson, Barrett, McGovern, Lloyd, Burns, O'Neill, Bowyer, Woodcock and Robertson."

That's how I found out I was playing in defence. No-one had said anything to me, I just took it from there that I was playing at the back and that was it. I had played in defence before, but not much. I never asked why I had been put there.

So we went on our pre-season trip to Germany, and got to the front desk of the hotel and who do I see giving out the room keys, but Clough himself, standing next to his family. "Room 214, Anderson and Woodcock," he said. "Room 215, Burns and Lloyd."

There were only about 15 of us in the squad, but we had a good camaraderie and started the season really well. We beat Everton away in our first league game and then faced Ipswich, whose captain Mick Mills said we were a team of has-beens. We spanked them 4-0.

We won the league in my first season there, in 1978. In those days, the gaffer wouldn't come into the dressing-room until quarter of an hour before kick-off. Clough would sit between me and Larry Lloyd before a game and drink a whiskey and light up a cigar. He would tell the substitute - whoever it was - to go and get him a whiskey, then he would get a huge cigar and blow smoke over Lloyd.

"For God's sake, boss," Lloyd would moan.

"I just do that to annoy the big bastard," he would say to me.

Then we just sat around and talked about anything: what we did last night, that kind of thing. The last thing he would always say was: "Right lads, get the ball, because if you've got the ball, they can't score." His philosophy was that simple.

The year before the final against Hamburg, we made our European debut. We had a first-round draw that we didn't want; against Liverpool. We wanted to play Real Madrid or Barcelona. A glamour tie. But Liverpool were the holders and were English. We would rather have gone abroad.

The first leg was at the City Ground, and Birtles got us the first goal. In the second half, Liverpool had a corner and we broke quickly. Birtles got the knock-down and laid it off to Colin Barrett, who had been called into the team. He smashed it in. That made it 2-0 and gave me the belief that we were through to the second round. We never conceded a lot of goals. We defended from the front and attacked from the back. And we knew we could beat Liverpool at their place because we'd done it in the league. We drove up for the second leg on the Wednesday morning, and we had some beers on the way up. Then we had a sleep in the afternoon and kept a clean sheet that night. That's how we knocked out Liverpool.

In the next round, we beat AEK Athens 2-1 at their place and won 5-1 at home. I had a cartilage injury so missed those games, and the ones against Grasshoppers, which we won 4-1 before a 1-1 draw. We could keep it tight at the back, but with Birtles, and John Robertson, Archie Gemmill and the like, we had a lot of players capable of scoring.

I was still out for the semi-final first leg against Cologne. That was at our place and it was difficult to watch: we drew 3-3. But after the game, Peter Taylor was ridiculously confident. His daughter lived in Germany and he had gone over there and seen a lot of their games. He knew they were a defensive-minded side and was adamant that we would win over there. He knew they wouldn't be going for it at home, and I think he even had a bet on us.

I was back for the return game and I loved it. Ian Bowyer scored a goal for us in the second half, and then they threw the kitchen sink at us. We held firm. I liked that game. It's not so enjoyable being a defender when there's nothing to do, and we really got stuck in.

Big Larry was superb that night. We just understood each other, we knew what we had to do. Good players know where to go and I like to think we were both good players. We worked in tandem: Larry always covered for me while I always covered for him. We were the heart of the team with John McGovern just in front of us. That triangle was very tight.

So we were in the final against Malmö, who were a poor team. They only ever won matches 1-0. We weren't the best team in the world, but we still had to beat them. Once again, on the way to the stadium in Munich, we had some beers on the coach. It was totally normal for us: if it was hot, the boss would say, "Have a beer and get some fluid into your body." Some teams still keep a bottle of whiskey in the dressing-room and have a nip of that. We had some beers and that was it.

We had two injury concerns: Martin O'Neill and Archie Gemmill had both missed some games. We trained on the day of the match and afterwards Clough said, "Martin, how is your hamstring feeling?"

Martin said, "It's fine, boss. I feel fine."

The boss then said, "Archie, how's your ankle?"

"Yes, it's fine now, thanks. I've been training for two weeks and I feel good," he replied.

"I'm delighted for the two of you," Clough said. "You're both sitting on the bench."

I don't think Martin or Archie ever forgave him for that. I certainly think Martin struggled to accept that decision. Trevor Francis made his European debut in the final in place of O'Neill. He had just moved to Forest from Birmingham, like me, but Trevor had become the first ever million pound transfer and so there was plenty of pressure on him to perform. Francis scored the only goal of the game - a diving far post header from John Robertson's cross.

Clough later called his decision to leave out O'Neill and Gemmill the hardest he ever had to make, but maybe it was the wrong decision. Yes, it got us the result, but I'm thinking of the impact it had long-term. Being fair to Martin, he would definitely have played had he been fit.

The Malmö game was a bit of an anti-climax as neither team were particularly well-known. We were presented with the cup, we did a lap of honour, and we got back into the dressing-room. The boss stood up and said, "I want all your medals, so put them on the table."

I thought, "Sod that, I'm keeping mine," so I put mine in my pocket.

The gaffer took the others. I think he wanted to get some copies made. Jimmy Gordon never got a medal and nor did Colin Barrett. Poor Colin, the week after he scored that crucial second goal against Liverpool, he was playing at Middlesbrough and he injured his cruciate ligament. It ended his career. He never got a medal and it niggled him that his goal set the whole thing up for us. His goal was a momentous part of that campaign.

Liverpool won the league that season. They were superb. They got 67 points and we got 60. But we qualified for the next season's European Cup as holders. That year we started against a Swedish side, Osters Vaxjo, and won 2-0 before drawing 1-1. We were back on the road, but very little had changed. We had brought in two new players, Gary Mills, a young forward who was only 17, and a defender, Bryn Gunn, who was 19.

Otherwise it was much the same. The build-up never changed, whether we were playing Hamburg or Grantham. The players had their own way of doing things and the coaches had theirs. Martin O'Neill used to put plasters on all his toes before every game. I liked to get ready 40 minutes before kick-off, with a cup of tea and a rub-down. Nothing special there. Peter Taylor liked to watch a horse-race and have a bet. The gaffer would speak to the press, or play with his kids in his office. Then, 15 or 20 minutes before the game, he would come into the changing-room and speak to us. We were never scared of him. We couldn't have done what we did if we had any fear. Everyone performs better when they are relaxed.

So the European adventure continued: we beat Arges Pitesti 2-0 and 2-1 and then had a tricky quarter-final against Dynamo Berlin. We lost the first leg 1-0 at home. Just like against Cologne, we needed to get a result away from home. I was suspended for the return game: everyone said I would get suspended all the time when I moved into defence and that was my first suspension in my third season at Forest. They may have thought they had done enough, by winning at our place, but we had goalscorers throughout the side. We were a capable team and won 3-1 over there, though I did not find it easy viewing!

The semi-final was against Ajax and I was back in the side. Trevor Francis was great that game, he was quick as lightning in the box and he snaffled a chance to put us ahead. It has been said that Trevor and I didn't get on, but we did. We just had our own group of friends. While he went flat-racing at Ascot, I would go to the dog-track at Milton Keynes. There was a bit of rivalry between us, whether it was playing the five-a-sides, or between Scotland and England, or whatever. But I had no real problems with him. He had ability, pace and could score.

John Robertson then got a penalty, he never missed from the spot, and we were 2-0 up. With that advantage, going to Amsterdam we felt really confident. I always remember Trevor had a great chance from four yards out in the second leg, but put his header over the bar. We lost 1-0, but held on to reach the final.

The boss took us away to Mallorca for the week before the game. He liked it there and we had a good time. We did a little bit of training, but we were mainly there to chill out. We did a bit of drinking, we went to pubs and clubs at night, but we just relaxed. It was a great week: we sunbathed, played tennis, sat by the pool, went for a meal, had some drinks and had a laugh. The manager always wanted us to be relaxed. Stan Bowles, who had played in the semi-final against Ajax, never turned up that week because he didn't like flying. That cost him his place in the final which went to young Gary Mills.

We visited the Bernabéu the day before the game and it was sensational. We had a walk around and it was really great. It felt like a crime to even walk on the pitch, it was so soft. It was definitely the best playing surface I have ever run on. We were staying in a hotel in the mountains. In our last training session on the morning of the game, there was a hailstorm during a five-a-side match. I said, "The next goal wins," and we were trying to let the boss score so we could get out of the hailstorm and get inside. That was the last time the gaffer ever played a five-a-side with us.

We never spoke about the opposition at any time - not even before the Hamburg game. We knew a few things: that Keegan would make it a battle; that they had a right-back, Kaltz, who liked to go forward; and they had a big centre-half that Larry or I had to watch at set-pieces. And they had the German international striker, Horst Hrubesch, who was on the bench as he had a supposed ankle injury. We called him Horst Rubbish.

We knew we had to be tough. We knew we would have to defend, but we didn't want to defend as much as we did. It was John Robertson who got our goal, quite early on it was. He cut in from his left flank and used his right foot to place a shot from outside the area right inside the goalkeeper's far post. Perfect placement.

As I have said, it suited us to defend a lead as we all defended throughout the team. Larry and I were confident that we could keep a clean sheet and as soon as we were ahead, I had a good feeling.

Peter Shilton had come in as our goalkeeper and I maintain that he never had that much to do. When someone shoots from 20 or 30 yards, the goalkeeper should save it. The shots that Shilts had to deal with against Malmö and Hamburg were all from distance and he did well. The thing with him was, he never came off his line. So if the ball was around the six-yard line, it was up to me to clear it. But Shilts was a very good shot-stopper. His reflexes were superb.

Credit to Hamburg as they pushed us back, but credit to us as we stopped them from scoring. Everyone played their heart out: from Robertson to young Gary Mills up front. Meanwhile Garry Birtles did more miles up front than Red Rum. We competed everywhere. We knew that one of us could score at any time, and we often scored and then kept a clean sheet.

Towards the end of the game, Frank Gray turned to me and said, "Burnsy, my calf is knackered."

I told the bench that Frank was finished, and was later told that Peter turned to Clough and said, "Who have we got?"

"We've got Gunny,' said Clough.

"Oh, then we're in the shit now," came the reply.

Gunny was shitting himself about coming on as he had very little experience. I remember he started to take off his tracksuit off, but he had his sleeve inside out and couldn't get his arm out because he was so nervous. As it happened, he played for the last ten minutes and strolled through it. By then, Hamburg had sent on that big lump Horst Rubbish, but he never beat Larry to a header.

So we won the trophy and ran to the end where the Forest fans were. They were throwing stuff, like scarves and shirts. Then someone threw a trumpet and it hit John McGovern on the head. John was interviewed on TV after the game and the interviewer said, "That's a nasty bruise, was that with a clash with one of the players?"

John said, "Yeah, I think so," because he didn't want to upset the fan that threw the trumpet onto the pitch. That was the kind of guy John was. There's a famous picture taken from the dressing-room after the game: we're all standing there, John Robertson has a towel round him, and none of us look very happy. The gaffer had just told us that we were not allowed to go out that night. We were only to go back to the hotel.

We got back to the hotel in the mountains, and the boss said, "Drink as much as you like, but stay in tonight." After a few hours, when it was about one in the morning, we were bored in the hotel bar, so we called for a taxi. A few of us went downtown: there was Larry, John Robertson, Viv Anderson, Martin O'Neill, and myself. We had some friends in town, and we went to see our wives and celebrated with them all.

We got a taxi back at around seven in the morning. The gaffer came down for breakfast a bit later and said, "You guys have been here all night then?" He must have known we'd been out, but he never said anything. I once saw him many years later and the first thing he said was, "You were one of those bastards who sneaked out after the game, weren't you?"

His man-management skills were superb. He expected you to behave like a professional and if you did, he would respect you and expect to get respect back. Sometimes we didn't see him all week. He may say on a Saturday, "Right, I don't want you to come in until Thursday." But as long as we did the business on the pitch, he was fine. Now it's all about ice-buckets after the game, warming down, and blood-thinning. We just used to have a cup of tea and John Robertson always liked a fag. The game has become a lot more serious now, but let's remember it's supposed to be fun.

I only stayed for one more season at the club. We played against Barcelona in the European SuperCup and beat them 1-0 at the City Ground and drew 1-1 at Camp Nou. I scored our goal that night, but I remember it more because at the final whistle, our chairman, a fat fellow called Mr McPherson, ran onto the pitch. He was hugging the players and having his picture taken with us for the papers. But the gaffer went crazy at us for letting him near us. "What the fuck is he doing in the pictures?" he raged. "If he ever does that again kick him out. He should not be there." Then we went to Tokyo for the World Club Championship, but we lost 1-0 to Nacional. Trevor Francis then left and I felt the team was breaking up. I asked for a move and Leeds came in for me. I spent a few years there, six months at Derby and then Leeds again.

The next time something momentous happened at Forest, it was 1993. I had retired by then, but was playing for the Forest Over-35s team, who were called the Shaggy Dogs. We were meeting at the City Ground on a Sunday morning and the day before, Forest had lost 2-0 to Sheffield United. It meant we had been relegated from the Premier League in its first year.

It was a sad morning for me. I walked round the pitch just remembering all the games I had played in. And I couldn't stop crying.

PAOLO ROSSI
FORWARD 1981–1985

BORN   23rd September 1956, Prato, Italy
SIGNED   1981 from Vicenza; £500,000
JUVENTUS CAREER   138 games, 44 goals
HONOURS   1 Italian Serie A League title, 1 Italian Cup, 1 European Cup,
1 European Cup Winners' Cup, 1 European SuperCup, 1 World Cup,
48 Italy caps, European Footballer of the Year 1982
LEFT   Transferred to AC Milan, July 1985

Paolo Rossi's career had the highest of highs and the lowest of lows. He began
at Juventus, but became known as a predatory goalscorer at Vicenza.
He played for Italy in the 1978 World Cup, but was banned for two years
after a match-fixing scandal in 1980, a charge that he always denied. Juventus
re-signed him mid-ban, an excellent piece of business as he finished top scorer
in the victorious 1982 World Cup campaign. He spent three successful seasons
in Turin, before moving to AC Milan and then Verona before retiring aged 31.
He now works as a pundit for Italian TV station Sky.

Juventus 1 v Liverpool 0

Wednesday 29 May 1985

Heysel Stadium, Brussels
Attendance 58,000

*Juventus win their first European Cup, but the game is overshadowed by the
deaths of 39 fans. English clubs are later banned from Europe for five years*

Teams

Stéfano Tacconi	1	Bruce Grobbelaar
Luciano Favero	2	Phil Neal
Antonio Cabrini	3	Jim Beglin
Sergio Brio	4	Mark Lawrenson
		(sub. Gary Gillespie)
Gaetano Scirea	5	Ronnie Whelan
Massimo Bonini	6	Alan Hansen
Marco Tardelli	7	Kenny Dalglish
Massimo Briaschi	8	Steve Nicol
(sub. Cesare Prandelli)		
Paolo Rossi	9	Ian Rush
(sub. Benjamino Vignola)		
Michel Platini	10	Paul Walsh
		(sub. Craig Johnston)
Zbigniew Boniek	11	John Wark

Platini (pen) 56   **Scorers**

Referee: Daina (Switzerland)

Even though it happened so many years ago, it's still painful for me to remember that night. For me it's a dark, horrible nightmare. It was a terrible defeat for everybody, for everything I have always thought football is: fun and joy. Maybe I was a bit naive, but I always thought football was just a game - of course, one surrounded by a lot of money and business, but at the end it remains a game. Just a game.

I don't like to talk about the 1985 European Cup final, because it means only the tragedy in Brussels. Nothing more. No Cup, no match, only an immense horror which killed so many innocent people. I can't be proud of having been there that night, even if the players can't be blamed for what happened. It's even too easy to say that if the peak of my career was the sensational hat-trick that dumped Brazil out of the 1982 World Cup, Heysel represents the saddest and deepest point.

It should have been the match of revenge for us, but it soon became a match of death. We were all looking forward to playing the final after what happened two years before in Athens, in 1983, when we were deservedly beaten by Hamburg. That was an incredible game. We were so much better than them, and not only on paper.

But one of the problems of that Juventus side was that sometimes we were too confident and we suffered a lack of focus. The run-up to the 1983 final was brilliant, we never lost a game and we played our best football. Remember in that team we had seven or eight players who were Italy internationals that had just won the World Cup. Additional value came from two fantastic foreign players, Michel Platini and Zbigniew Boniek. There was a mix of old and young players, so many talents, all in one team. It was amazing to play with them. I really enjoyed playing during that period, not only because we won most of our games, but also because we had a positive approach. There were so many big names in the squad, but no rivalries, which is quite rare in a dressing-room. We all felt the same commitment: the tremendous desire to win. There was no room for any other feeling. I can't say we were close friends off the pitch, but when we were on it, it was natural to help each other achieve our common goal. I played together for so many years with these guys that we were a real group, we shared the same winning mentality.

I was lucky to be part of that Juventus side, because I was coming out of a terrible two-year ban for match-fixing while on loan at Perugia, something which I will always deny. Juventus had bought me back from Vicenza for a cut-price fee, after selling me to them for a world record £1.75m, two months before the 1982 World Cup, just when the ban had been lifted. I only played a few matches before that tournament.

But even now I thank two people who always trusted me: Italy's coach Enzo Bearzot and Juventus manager Giovanni Trapattoni. Bearzot was almost fired for selecting me for the World Cup. No-one in Italy expected him to pick me and to be honest, I also doubted my chances due to lack of match fitness. In the early stages of the competition it looked like Bearzot had made a terrible mistake. I failed to score in Italy's first four matches. The press called for me to be dropped. A few years later, Bearzot told me that he remembered my contribution to the last World Cup campaign when I played alongside Roberto Bettega, and scored three goals. He wanted to have an opportunist in the penalty box. I was always pretty good in that area, fast enough to exploit an attack. He never put responsibility on my shoulders, but I knew he expected things from me. This was an extra motivation in Spain because I could feel his support.

Trapattoni was really important to me during the long months of my suspension. It is hard to train day after day, week after week knowing you are not going to play on the Sunday. It was like time couldn't go fast enough. I used to count the hours before my return every day. I was in the middle of my career, about 24 years-old. There were days when it was difficult even to go to training because of how depressed I felt. But even though I wasn't playing, Trapattoni never let me down. That's his best quality: he made all the members of the team feel important and involved in the project which, in his case, involved only one thing: to win.

When I signed for Juventus, even though I couldn't play in Serie A matches, he used to stay after training and work on different exercises with me and the other substitutes. He had the unique ability to manage the dressing-room perfectly: he could be very friendly, but tough when necessary. He had an incredible determination which he transmitted to everyone. He used to play with us in the 11 v 11 training games and always wanted to mark Michel Platini. Because players didn't give 100 per cent in those games, Trapattoni couldn't stop running and beating him. For Michel, it was torture because he couldn't even complain!

Despite the long suspension, my career changed drastically after the World Cup. It exploded. Not only because my exploits earned me a place in football history, but also because my confidence increased enormously. I had played for the national team at the 1978 World Cup in Argentina, but after two years of my ban, my self-confidence was low.

Juventus rebuilt my personality, feeding my will to win. I know there is nothing greater than a World Cup for a player, but if you don't confirm your abilities at your club, you feel you are missing something. That's what happened to me. It's also why clever players don't only follow the money, but also try to join a winning club.

The reason why we lost the 1983 final against Hamburg is quite simple: we didn't play the right game mentally. Before the match we were too calm and relaxed, pretty sure we were going to win. No-one said it openly, but our self-confidence was too high. Our presumptuousness cost us the trophy. We came up against a mentally stronger team who wanted to win more than us. They were hungrier and they fully deserved the win. When you start a match with the wrong attitude, it's almost impossible to change it. They scored an early goal and that just showed us the huge mistake we had made. There were no excuses, and no reaction. It was possibly one of the games when I ran the most in my career, but it was meaningless. We were all so confused that I remember no-one spoke at half-time.

Despite such a terrible experience, we understood our mistake straight after the match, and promised ourselves that we would win that competition soon. You can say that the seeds to the 1985 final were sowed two years earlier in that Greek dressing-room. We never mentioned the defeat by Hamburg again even if we couldn't stop thinking about it, almost every day for those two years.

That was the real secret of our wonderful team: from the goalkeeper, Dino Zoff, to the last substitute, we all desperately wanted to win every game, against every team. In the Athens silence we realised that we could have played that final again, and we would have won it. So from the next day, we set about our work just aiming to win the European Cup. Trapattoni was so worried about our only thought, to win that cup, that he thought it had become an obsession. Sometimes, especially before international games, he used to say, "You can't always win. In sport, it's important to be able to accept defeat."

No way, not with that group of people, who always wanted trophies. In the Juventus dressing-room, there were big stars, but no-one was the real leader, not even Platini, who was charismatic and a fantastic player. In his first three years at Juventus he was amazing, but life wasn't exactly easy for him.

In his first season, Platini topped the Serie A scoring charts as he did in each of the next two years. All the media attention was on him. But Marco Tardelli, whenever he went into the dressing-room, always used to shout in Michel's face, "Always remember lad, I won the World Cup. Not you." It was meant as a joke, but it explains the high quality of that dressing-room, with so many successful players.

The 1985 run to the final was brilliant, despite a close shave in the semi-final second leg at Bordeaux. We had won the first leg 3-0 in Turin and we thought we had already reached the final. It was another big mistake that almost cost us dear. In France we were very lucky to only lose 2-0, because we played really badly.

We under-estimated our opponents. We always used to respect the team we were playing against, but sometimes our own confidence caused us problems.

Personally I used to love playing in the European Cup. The domestic league was the routine, but the European matches were always an event. We played at night, and they were shown live on TV. I was not the only one to feel the special charm of these matches. Boniek loved playing in Europe so much that he used to play so much better in these games. The Juventus owner, Gianni Agnelli, used to call him '*Beau de la Nuit*' due to his confidence in the evening fixtures.

I like the current format of the Champions League, but the challenge of knock-out matches is more fascinating, more exciting than a group stage. Every year there were lots of surprises and it was almost impossible to predict what would happen. I also think that the team who wins the competition nowadays is absolutely the best in Europe, but in the past I'm not sure it was the same.

When we knew we would be facing Liverpool in the final, we were excited. We had already beaten them a few months earlier in the European SuperCup in Turin. We knew them quite well and were pretty sure we could beat them again. It was our typical attitude, respecting the team but never being worried. We felt we were one of the best European sides, maybe even the best one. We needed to confirm it on the pitch, but in our mind we knew it was the right time. The year before we had won the European Cup Winners' Cup quite easily.

In the days before the match in Brussels, Trapattoni was working more on motivation than tactics. We were a very solid team, we didn't change our system because of the opponents. We played four at the back, with left-back Antonio Cabrini often helping the attack. In midfield there was only one defensive player who was Massimo Bonini, plus Marco Tardelli who used to score lots of goals. Helping up front were two creative players like Massimo Briaschi and Platini with two strikers, Boniek and myself. I don't think we had any weakness, in every part of the pitch we were the best. It's wrong to accuse this side of playing *catenaccio*. We were pragmatic and we knew when to defend a result. We were dedicated to winning games, that's true, and not necessarily entertaining people. But that's what football is, and our supporters agreed: they wanted to win trophies as much as us. And they understood if sometimes to win a game we had to play poorly. The result was not the most important thing in football, but the only important thing. At least I thought so.

I remember the day before the game, when we had our last training-session at the Heysel Stadium, we were all surprised about the condition of the ground. None of us had ever played in Brussels before then and we discovered it was old and crumbling. But to be honest, we didn't care too much. We were focused on the game, desperate not to miss another opportunity to win our place in European history.

The team was calm. Trapattoni made a short speech when we went back to the hotel, trying to relax the few of us who were nervous. He explained the tactics he wanted: the plan was to wait early on for the Liverpool assault and try to score on the counter-attack. Quite simple. His main concern was that our team be concentrated on the match from the first minute. The Athens memory still hurt all of us.

I was never too worried before a game, even before the World Cup final. It's about character, and I'm always calm and I never had any problems sleeping in these situations. I used to share my room with Cabrini, one of my best friends in football, because we had pretty similar characters and the same habits. We stayed in our room as much as we could by ourselves, playing music and cards and talking a lot. Tardelli was totally different to us, he couldn't ever sleep before the big games. Never. Before the World Cup final, Bearzot's assistant, Cesare Maldini, had to spend the whole night with him, trying to calm him down. But he couldn't. In Brussels I can't remember which Juventus director sacrificed his night for this special duty.

We had watched a few Liverpool match videos the day before and what impressed us was their physical strength and their ability with the long-ball game. But the night before, I didn't talk to Cabrini about Liverpool or the final. As usual, we played cards for a while and went to bed. I never dream and that night it was the same. Maybe it happens sometimes, but I can never remember. As I think back now to the build-up to the game, it doesn't seem so different from other ones. All our players had international experience and were pretty used to that kind of pressure.

Juventus hadn't ever won the European Cup, which was bizarre for the most successful Italian team domestically. But we players didn't care too much about that, because despite the Athens defeat we always did quite well in the other competitions. It was the board who cared more about winning in Europe. Only two Italian teams, AC Milan and Internazionale, had won the European Cup, both twice, and the club used to feel we needed to win it to be considered the best Italian club. They wanted to be proud to confirm that we were the best in Italy, and had become the first European side to lift all three Uefa trophies.

Saying that, when a club reaches two finals within three years, they have done a fantastic job, even if you end up losing both of them, like Juventus did in the late-1990s. A final is always unpredictable. You never know what will happen. You need to be lucky to win. And I was almost 29 years-old, with a long career behind me. I was ready to cope with the expectation. When you play and win a World Cup, everything else is in a different perspective. You realise you have achieved a peak, done the best you can, and all the rest is just a bonus. I'm not saying that I didn't care any more, not at all, but it was a different feeling. I wasn't scared any more.

When you play for Juventus, you have to give 100 per cent in every game to confirm your qualities. It's about their tradition, their honour, the name of the club: it's something you learn the first day after you sign. You can't hide and live in your past with that shirt. The rules were strict in that era. It was called 'Juventus style', a mix of rules of behaviour on and off the pitch. The president, Giampiero Boniperti, was a former Juventus legend who wanted to know everything about the players' personal lives. The first thing Platini had to do when he joined us was cut his hair. He didn't want to, but he had to. Boniperti was also obsessed with marriage. He wanted all the players to be married so, in his opinion, they would spend more time at home with family. When Gaetano Scirea went to his office to tell him he was getting married, Boniperti proposed himself to be the best man. And when your President makes you an offer like that, you can't say no!

Boniperti was also in charge of contracts and it was really tough to deal with him. You could earn more playing for a different club, but Juventus meant prestige and trophies. That's why, even now, the club is first choice for almost all Italian players. Playing for them automatically elevates you as one of the best players of your generation. But Turin helped me not only as a footballer, but also to mature as a man.

I learned my trade at Juventus though when I celebrated my 18th birthday, I had problems with my cartilages, which were removed from both knees, and I was sent to Como. I made my name at Vicenza, but I always considered myself a Juventus player. So you can imagine my happiness when Juventus brought me back at the worst moment of my career, during my suspension. They paid me almost nothing, so you could say that no other club had done a better deal. Anyway, the bad experience of my suspension had forced me to open my eyes and be more careful in my life. I lost two important seasons in my career and I can't forgive myself for that even if I did so well in the following season. Maybe that's the reason why I didn't waste time and felt the same will to win as players like Dino Zoff, Claudio Gentile, Tardelli and Scirea. It was an attitude we had.

When we arrived at the Heysel Stadium, two-and-a-half hours before the game, the atmosphere inside was quite calm. The stands were already packed, and when we walked onto the pitch, we went and greeted our fans. After that, we went back to the dressing-room, thinking ahead, thinking only of the final.

As usual, before every big game there was a heavy silence in the room. I was not superstitious, but I always went through the same routine before a game: opening my bag in the same way, sitting next to the same team-mate. While you wait before a final, the room becomes claustrophobic. You want to go out and run around the pitch. The tension takes your breath away and you need to empty that feeling as soon as possible.

As usual, I was one of the first to start warming up. It was 30 minutes before kick-off, while we were finishing our warm-up, when the first news came to us. We weren't told exactly what was going on in the stands. We knew there were some fights, and possibly that one person had died, but no-one explained to us that so many people had been killed. It's not like today when you can know almost everything in a few seconds. The internet and mobile phone had yet to arrive and we couldn't get a decent picture.

Maybe now I would appear very cynical, but think of it in this way: in a few minutes we were supposed to play one of the most important games of our career, a game we had always dreamt of playing. We were professionals and always tried our best, and focused on the game. The tension before such an important game, added to the confusion around the lack of information we were getting, combined to create a strange feeling in those first minutes. When a UEFA official told us about the first delay, for 15 minutes, I became a little more nervous. I was being pulled between two different tensions: on one side I had, and I wanted, to play a really important final, but on the other side, there was clearly something wrong, which I didn't know about, which was happening outside and I was a bit scared.

Even if my relatives weren't in the stands, most of my team-mates had wives or children out there. And you could see the deep concern on their faces. But I never thought that we wouldn't have played the game, because I couldn't ever have imagined the tragedy that came. So I tried to stay isolated for a few minutes to get concentrated. I remember some players tried to call their families to find out more. Some Italian journalists tried to run into our dressing-room, they wanted to speak with us. They weren't allowed in.

Minute after minute we were growing more and more uncomfortable. We didn't really know what was going on, but the suspicion that there was trouble affected us. We wanted to know more, but no-one answered our questions. Even Boniek, one of the funniest guys in the squad who always used to joke before every game, was completely silent. His face was pale, he couldn't stop talking to the referee and UEFA officials. Nobody wanted to give him the full picture.

Finally, a journalist from Turin came where we were - half of us were in the tunnel, half still in the dressing-room - and he told us that there had been trouble in a Liverpool stand, but all our relatives were fine. I remember him explaining that, because even for the media, at that moment, the full scale of the tragedy that had actually occured wasn't yet clear. We were ready to play, but delay followed delay and the match was postponed for 90 minutes. In the dressing-room, we were more and more on edge.

Just before the game, someone suggested that not one, but two Juventus supporters had died. We didn't know how to take that. The news wasn't clear and we still hadn't been given a final decision on whether to play or not. We could have risked a long suspension from UEFA, or a fine from our club: but more important to us at that time was finding someone we could believe.

There was so much confusion we couldn't have taken any reasonable decision. We were the worst people to have to make a decision because our minds were not with us, they were focused on the game.

I think the final responsibility on whether to play or not came down to the UEFA directors. So when they decided to play the game, we accepted it. None of us said it would have been better not to play. We didn't discuss the decision as a group, although some of us briefly mentioned it. The Belgian and UEFA officials received some blame later. I didn't say a word at the time, but I still believe it was the right decision.

Once we got on the pitch, when the referee started the game, the final against Liverpool was strange, uncomfortable. But it's not true to say it wasn't a real game. I wasn't in the heads of the Liverpool players, but my impression is that they gave 100 per cent and tried to win the game.

The tackles were hard as usual, as was their effort to equalise our goal. I never took the opportunity to talk to them after the game. It may not seem so important now to see if it was a real final or not from a sporting point of view, but my impression is that it was. When Platini scored the winning goal, the only goal of the game, from the penalty spot, for example, we celebrated it as usual. The same for Liverpool: they protested the penalty decision. Now, I don't know what to think about our celebrations. I felt mixed emotions: tension, rage and also happiness. I can't deny that I feel a bit embarrassed for that happiness. Someone accused us of having danced over the bodies of 39 dead fans. That was an infamous charge which I firmly reject.

We wanted to win, that's true. We wanted to win for us, firstly, but also for our families and our supporters. We played to win as Liverpool did. But we didn't lack respect on the pitch for the simple reason that we practically didn't know anything. I'll never get tired of repeating that.

A few years later Platini said that we were like the clown in the circus who is sent on stage after the trapeze artist has failed and I agree with that. It wasn't a beautiful game, and I didn't play particularly well, but as I said before, I don't really like to remember that night, because it meant nothing in the face of such a tragedy.

The UEFA officials gave us the trophy in the dressing-room, but we decided to go back onto the pitch to show it to our supporters. Maybe we were naive because we wanted to bring them some joy after what had happened before the game. We thought it would have been more disrespectful to have not done that. I swear that we still had no idea of how many people had died. Of course we wouldn't ever have done it had we had known the scale of the disaster.

It was only when we went back to the hotel and switched on the TV did we find out about the full impact of the tragedy. It was really late when we left Heysel after the press conference, and we all were tired, emotionally more than physically. I was just looking forward to going to bed and sleeping. I couldn't cope any more with all the tension.

As soon as we reached the hotel we all ate something in the restaurant and ran to our rooms. I watched the Belgian news reports. I could barely understand anything, but kept on watching. Many people still think that the final should not have been played, but I don't agree. Everyone who was there that night remembers the tension in the air. The police authorities asked us to play, as did UEFA. The major concern was that the situation could have been exacerbated. Something even worse could have happened. The police actually thought that the game would distract the hooligans.

Twenty years after the event, the strongest feeling I have is a huge sense of incredulity. Even today, it is hard to accept that someone can die because of a game of football you played in. It's unbelievable. I still pray for the families of the victims every night. And after what happened, that trophy has no meaning for me. In my career I won an Italian Cup, a national league title, a Cup Winners' Cup, a World Cup - but not the European Cup. I erased that from my memory.

Sometimes professional footballers are accused of being insensitive, but it wasn't the case. Once I spoke to Platini's wife, who told me that Michel wanted to give everything up. In his head was the fact that a Frenchman, who died at Heysel, had come to see him play. That broke Michel in two. And it was the same for every member of that team. I think it is sad that the unfair sacrifice of those people forced the whole world of football to improve their stadiums and increase their levels of security.

I don't think there was only one thing responsible for the Heysel tragedy. The English supporters who attacked the Italians started everything off. But the people who gave them the chance to do that are also guilty. When you look at Heysel, you realise how much the football world has changed and improved in the last two decades. There were only a few policemen at that stadium that night, and even though it was one of the most important sporting events of the year, the infrastructure in place was so poor. I can't understand why UEFA chose Heysel for such a high profile game.

But having said that, I still never thought a tragedy like that could happen, even if the fence was pathetic and we knew Liverpool supporters at that time had a bad reputation. After that night, after everyone watched the awful scenes as they happened, football changed a lot. We had experienced the wild side of the game and it was like the dream was over.

I played for few years after that, but at Milan I was a sort of shadow of myself. Injuries had returned to plague me, just as they did when I was a teenager. And I couldn't play anymore at my best level. But I don't think it's wrong to think that my real career ended that night. I never forgot the memory of what happened in Brussels. But I've never gone back since then. I don't think I could cope with such an emotional return.

MAURO TASSOTTI
RIGHT-BACK 1980–1997

BORN   19th January 1960, Rome
SIGNED   1980 from Lazio
AC MILAN CAREER   424 games, 8 goals
HONOURS   5 Italian League titles, 4 Italian SuperCups, 3 European Cups, 2 Intercontinental Cups, 3 European SuperCups, 31 Italy caps
LEFT   Retired, May 1997

Mauro Tassotti was an uncompromising defender who feared his best days were behind him when Arrigo Sacchi was appointed Milan coach in 1987. But Tassotti blossomed under Sacchi and became an integral part of Milan's triple European Cup-winning side. Uefa's Technical Study Group voted him the best right-back ever to have played in the Champions League. After his retirement in 1997, he worked at Milanello and was briefly Milan co-coach with Cesare Maldini in 2001, guiding the team to a famous 6-0 win over Inter. He is currently AC Milan's assistant coach.

AC Milan 4 v Steaua Bucharest 0

Wednesday 24 May 1989

Camp Nou, Barcelona
Attendance 94,000

*AC Milan begin a cycle of success under president Silvio Berlusconi, winning
the first of three European Cups in six years. Coach Arrigo Sacchi is credited
with introducing an attacking style to the Italian side*

Teams

Giovanni Galli	1	Silviu Lung
Mauro Tassotti	2	Dan Petrescu
Paolo Maldini	3	Stefan Iovan
Alessandro Costacurta	4	Adrian Bumbescu
(sub. Filippo Galli)		
Franco Baresi	5	Nicolae Ungureanu
Angelo Colombo	6	Daniel Minea
Frank Rijkaard	7	Gheorghe Hagi
Carlo Ancelotti	8	Iosif Rotariu
		(sub. Gavril Balint)
Marco Van Basten	9	Tudorel Stoica
Ruud Gullit	10	Marius Lacatus
(sub. Pietro Paolo Virdis)		
Roberto Donadoni	11	Victor Piturca

Gullit, 17, 38 **Scorers**
Van Basten 26, 46

Referee: Tritschler (West Germany)

It all started with a defeat. In life, there is no joy without a struggle, and the same is true in sport. To win, you need first to taste defeat. In this case, it happened just a few months after Arrigo Sacchi took over as coach in 1987. We lost 2-0 to Espanyol in the second round of the UEFA Cup. Sacchi wasn't well known even in Italy back then and it was a huge surprise when our President, Silvio Berlusconi, appointed him. Not only had he never played as a professional footballer, but he had never coached in Serie A.

I was surprised when I first met him. Milan were not one of the best Italian sides then, but we had a great tradition. We had qualified for the UEFA Cup and were looking to improve the side using Berlusconi's money and ambition. There were already some excellent players in the team - like Franco Baresi, Carlo Ancelotti, Ruud Gullit and Marco van Basten - but Sacchi treated us like a team of youngsters who needed to learn how to play. He was explaining to these legends, all players with prestigious careers, where to stand on the pitch, when to attack and when to defend.

For the first time in my life, I was working with a guy who told me what to do without the ball, and how to create space for team-mates. It was totally different to what I was used to and it wasn't easy to understand what he wanted. There were two reasons: one was because his tactical system was new for us. The other was that I was already 27 and that's not the ideal age to change your style of play. To explain his ideas, he showed us thousands of videotapes of Parma, his former club who were in Serie B. Can you imagine the reaction of Italy internationals, or people like Gullit, being told to spend hours in front of the TV watching a bunch of unknowns and learning how to play? It was pretty bizarre, but Sacchi was sure of himself.

We soon started calling him *Il Martello*, 'The Hammer', because he never stopped giving us orders. There were instructions on and off the pitch. Sacchi was always the first to arrive at the training-centre at Milanello and always the last to leave. If anyone stayed behind for extra training, he would teach them something new.

I was once injured and was on a different training schedule. I was the only one left on the pitches and it was pouring with rain. I was heading back to the changing-room, but before I got there, Sacchi stopped me. He spent ten minutes explaining some defensive moves to me by putting little stones on the ground and moving them round. I was soaking wet. I was freezing cold. But I couldn't stop him. He was desperate to explain this stuff to me.

That was just one example of his enthusiasm to teach us. The night before every game, he used to come to our rooms to speak to us and underline our duties for the next day. It was the first time in my career that the coach decided who roomed with whom. It was goalkeeper with goalkeeper, and defender with defender, simply to save him time when he did his rounds. He never focused too much on our opponents, he preferred us to concentrate on our own performances. He didn't care who he was talking to: everyone had the same duties and he just didn't want to repeat himself over and over.

I owe him a great debt because he changed my career and made me a much better player. I always thought I was a good professional, but I got better. I was only 21 when I moved from Lazio to Milan and I was expecting to win trophies because Milan were a big side. But when I got there, it was one of the worst spells in the club's history, and we were relegated twice in three seasons in the early 1980s - astonishing to think now. I always gave my best on the pitch and I should say that I did learn things from my first coach at Milan, Nils Liedholm.

But it was nothing compared to what happened under Sacchi. I remember the incredible effort he demanded in training, and the physical and mental fatigue from so many hours at work. We had never trained so hard, but the intensity of those sessions was vital for our style of play. There was little room for joking around. When I went home, I was so tired all I wanted to do was go to bed.

Sacchi's arrival meant a change for all of us, but you can see that his revolution worked as his legacy continues at Milan today. Coaches have come and gone since him, but the club always return to that style. Players like Paolo Maldini and Alessandro Costacurta, who were there then and are still now, represent Sacchi's vision of how football should be played. He was such a perfectionist, so painstaking, that it's hard to remember all his new ideas: nutrition was important, and so was the dynamic in the dressing-room. He was curious to know what we thought about his ideas. He would talk a lot with the players, but not just discussing tactics. He wanted to know everything about our private life, what we liked, where we went out at night.

We were quite impressed when he first arrived but we were never sure his methods would really improve our game. We understood the intensity of the training, but you can only tell how well you're doing out on the pitch. The Italian media, which is still very conservative, started a campaign against us because they thought we wanted to change the Italian style of play. That was true, but we didn't know if it would be possible. We supported the boss because we were seduced by his desire to show a different image to our football.

But after a horrible home defeat to Fiorentina and that UEFA Cup loss to Espanyol, it seemed that Sacchi would be sacked sooner rather than later. Often in Italy a club sacks its coach at the first sign of problems. But not this time: the Milan board backed Sacchi and that sent a message to us. We had to start believing in his new vision. The board was convinced, and therefore we were, that he would be a success.

Our season turned around the week after the Espanyol game. We beat Verona away, a tough game, and we were back. The new era was well and truly underway that January when we beat Napoli, Diego Maradona's Napoli, 5-1. It was important for our Scudetto hopes, but it was also a lesson in football: a team based on the great talent of a few players, Napoli, had been beaten by a collective where everyone knew where to go and what to do. Despite our poor start to the season, a few weeks before the end of the season we went to Napoli, the league leaders, needing a win to overtake them. We won, and in such a way that even the Napoli fans clapped us off the pitch.

The Scudetto was important, but as soon as Berlusconi arrived, he had wanted Milan to become the best team in the world. His horizons went beyond Italy, beyond Europe: he wanted the world. We knew our style of play would succeed in Europe and we were infected by his ambition. If it could work in Italy, especially in away games there, it could work in Europe. So the next season, we began the European campaign with no fears.

Sacchi would always repeat two things to us: the first was before the game, he only wanted us to talk about our performance and not our opponents. He didn't care if they were doing well or not, or if they played with one striker or two. We had to focus on ourselves. The second thing was the start of the game. Before he came, we used to start a game carefully, just wanting to keep the ball. He was completely against that: the first passage of play should always be going forward, not backwards. He didn't care if we lost possession: more important was to send a message to the opposition.

There was one game which started with us passing the ball back to our goalkeeper Giovanni Galli in three passes. Sacchi started shouting so loudly from the sidelines that the referee looked at him like he was crazy. "Attack from the start," was the message he had preached in training to us. And just once, we had forgotten it. This attacking principle was the main characteristic of that side, and it was unusual for an Italian side: we used to play the same away as at home, always wanting to win. We got rid of the 'draw culture', which is common with Italian teams away from home. The club philosophy under Berlusconi was to win, and play good football; to be spectacular, and to be aggressive; and to entertain our fans, and those of the opposition. It was strange. We were dominating the league, but for the first time people admired us rather than hated us.

Our first game in Europe that campaign was away at Levski Sofia. We won the game 2-0 and that gave a strong message. We had high expectations: for most of us it was our European Cup debuts, and it was only the first round, but we had targeted a place in the final even back then.

Sacchi always used to say, "You can't do anything in life without *occhio, pazienza e fortuna* (meaning, 'brains, patience and good luck'). The wisdom of his words was clear in the second round against Red Star Belgrade. I felt we were the better side, but we only drew the first game at the San Siro. They went ahead in the second leg before the referee disallowed a perfectly good goal for us. It was one of those games where you feel like you are never going to score. Suddenly a huge fog covered the pitch and the referee suspended the game. I will admit as soon as we realised there was a chance for that to happen, we pushed the referee to call it off. The Red Star players were complaining to the referee as we walked off the pitch.

That night I felt a lot of pressure. Sacchi relaxed the team, but later he came into the room I shared with Paolo Maldini. He admitted that during the game, he thought we were going to be knocked out of the competition. It seemed unbelievable for him to say such a thing, as he was always so confident about winning. I got more nervous and couldn't sleep that night. I didn't want us to blow our second chance. Suddenly we had more responsibility.

The next day, we dominated the game. But we lost Roberto Donadoni, who was an important player for us, through injury. The match went to penalties and we ended up winning.

I don't mind admitting we got lucky against Red Star, but what champion side is ever unlucky? It's part of the game. We were so tired, we couldn't train after the game. We lost our next league match, but the win in Belgrade had strengthened our resolve. Our group had become closer.

The previous summer I had played in the 1988 Olympics while Marco van Basten and Ruud Gullit had won the European Championships with Holland. They were the leaders of that great Dutch team, but their talent never affected their relationship with us. They were part of the team. Van Basten was a bit surprised that he had to train just the same as the rest of us. He missed a lot of games in his first season through injury, but once he was fit, he was one of the best in the world. He scored so many goals. There were times when he moaned to Sacchi because he felt he deserved preferential treatment. He never got any. For Sacchi, Van Basten may have been a special player, but he was just another member of the team and nothing more.

Sacchi used to explain the importance of being a role model as a footballer. Once, Van Basten scored and went to celebrate in the face of his marker, Pasquale Bruno, who had been kicking him all game. Sacchi immediately substituted him because of that celebration. I heard that a few years later, Van Basten asked Berlusconi to sell him to another club because his relationship with Sacchi was poor. Berlusconi was Van Basten's biggest fan. So he kept the Dutchman and sacked Sacchi.

In that season, we had already dropped a few points in the league so by winter it was clear that Europe was the priority. We were drawn to play Werder Bremen, the German champions, and they were tough. We struggled against teams that defended deep. And with the knock-out format as it was, when one mistake could cost you dear, there was always a risk. I think the current Champions League format makes it harder to win, with the best teams usually reaching the final, but the previous format was more exciting. Nowadays, you can make a mistake in the group stage and have time to recover. We couldn't then: but we won 1-0 on aggregate and were through to the semi-final.

We were up against Real Madrid, and the first leg at the Santiago Bernabéu was one of the best games Milan ever played. We did not win - it ended 1-1 - but we dominated the game from start to finish. Van Basten scored a fantastic goal, but more than that, an Italian side had imposed themselves in Madrid. We were disappointed that it was only a draw, but that summed up this Milan side. We wanted to win, even away at Real Madrid. We knew we deserved to win, and when we watched the video, it felt like we had won. We had proved in Europe what we had been showing in Italy, that we could dominate any team. That was our mission statement, and we had confirmed it at the home of Real Madrid. It was a good feeling. Their players congratulated us after the game, and that was pleasing. They were impressed, but even they didn't predict what would happen in the return game at the San Siro two weeks later.

We simply destroyed the myth of Real Madrid. We won 5-0. If the victory over Napoli the season before had given us confidence to believe in ourselves, this gave us even more strength. Beating Real Madrid 5-0 is a once-in-a-lifetime achievement. And we deserved it.

Our spirits were high the next day, but Sacchi was unmoved. He didn't celebrate in the dressing-room with us and though he was happy, he was already thinking about our opponents in the final: Steaua Bucharest. When we got to Milanello the day after that second leg, all the videotapes were waiting for us. Sacchi had studied our next opponents, even before the Real Madrid game. He knew everything about them. Steaua were a good team, but we weren't that impressed. We knew we could beat them.

Sacchi was obsessed with football: *Il Martello* spent all his time watching videos, talking about football, studying the game. The day before the final he told us to play our game as we had been, to change nothing. He put up old newspaper articles around the dressing-room, and he read aloud the most critical comments while we sat in silence. I never took any notice of criticism as I knew when I had played well or not. But Sacchi wanted that challenge with the press: they had been sceptical when he took over and this was his chance to prove himself.

Most of our fans had not seen the team win the previous European Cups, back in 1963 and 1969. And ten years earlier we had been relegated twice. The final was arranged for Camp Nou at Barcelona and we knew that Milan fans had bought most of the tickets because it wasn't easy to leave Romania back then. We knew our fans were passionate and loyal, but nothing prepared us for the sight when the team bus got to the stadium. Everywhere, there were fans in red. It was like a giant red sea. I can still remember getting goose-bumps when I realised how many fans were there for us. Even Gullit, one of the jokers of the team who was only ever quiet when Sacchi was talking in the dressing-room, was stunned into silence.

It was even more emotional when we warmed up for the first time. It was two hours before kick-off. The stadium was full of fans, all wearing red. Steaua had about 2,000 fans and the rest, around 80,000, were supporting us. I felt a huge pressure on my shoulders, but it soon lifted.

I was doing my exercises with Maldini and I thought back to the previous night, when Sacchi had come to our room to repeat his usual demands. It was the same before every match: he wanted me to support our attacking effort, always running just behind the midfielders. I had to stay around 20 yards behind Donadoni throughout the match, to cut the distance between the two lines. Maldini had to do the same on the other wing.

Maldini and me talked once Sacchi had left. I didn't like to talk when I felt under pressure, but that night I couldn't resist. I remembered my frustration as I had been with Milan for so many years when they had won nothing. I was partly to blame, because as I said, before Sacchi I had probably given only 60 per cent of what I could. But now I felt at my best. Maldini was still so young and had his career in front of him: I explained that I had no regrets, but wished I had been born a bit later so I could enjoy more of this success. Maldini was incredibly calm that night. Maybe it was because he was the son of Cesare Maldini, a great foot-baller and coach (who I worked with for a few months), but as soon as he got into the first-team, he behaved like a veteran. He was always in control. I was so impressed by him. I soon calmed down, because I didn't want him to get worried that night.

Before the game we ate some Mediterranean food, and also a slice of fruit-cake. The nutritionist used to advise us against eating sweet things before we played, but Sacchi, usually so tough and demanding, was a bit softer when it came to that.

We couldn't wait to play the game. We couldn't wait to win. The dressing-rooms at the Camp Nou are so far from the pitch, that we couldn't hear our fans chanting. But we had already seen the stands full of supporters and we knew what to expect once the game started. We were not hoping to win, we were expecting it, and the fans were the same. It was as though we were playing at the San Siro.

As soon as the game began, any nerves we had disappeared. From the first minute, we played our best football. It was a demonstration of the great confidence we had gained, starting from the win against Napoli and carrying on with the two great performances against Real Madrid. We were so superior that night that if we had played them ten times, we would have won every time. Even if you never quite know in football, I know we were a lot better than them. In a 20-minute spell in the first half, we had scored three goals - two from Gullit and one from Van Basten - and we could have scored more.

If there is such a thing as a perfect game, this was it: eleven players at their best, playing as a team, defending together and attacking together. This was the fruit of Sacchi's hard labour. He got the best out of every player. We knew what we had to do and we did it. In the build-up, Sacchi had focused on tactics because he did not want us to think about the game emotionally. He wanted us to play with intensity and courage, and to win with style. I was used to being told to win, but never to play well. The culture of results was the most important thing in Italy: no-one will ever criticise a winning team. But we changed that mentality. Now an Italian team could play with no fear, and could achieve the impossible. I knew we had the game in the bag once that third goal went in. We were so far ahead of them, but we were also playing so well, enjoying our football. It's not often you get that pure pleasure from playing, but that night, in a game footballers dream of playing in, we were enjoying ourselves. It was a sensational feeling.

No-one said a word at half-time. That was the rule: only Sacchi was allowed to speak. I was thrilled by the score-line, but to hear Sacchi speak, we could have been drawing or even losing. He repeated what we had to do, underlining all our jobs and highlighting the few mistakes we had made in the first half. His message was clear: there was still 45 minutes left, we still had to play well, keep attacking and try and score more goals. He told us to forget about the advantage we had.

His training sessions had made us so fit that when the match restarted we had no problems carrying out his orders. The first half went by very quickly and was dramatic, but the second was slower and calmer. I knew we had won, but didn't say a word until it was over. Even when Van Basten scored a fourth goal one minute after the break, I just celebrated as usual with my fellow defenders.

At the end, my own joy was overwhelmed by that of our supporters. Until then I had tried not to look at them too much because I wanted to focus on the game. But after the match, I celebrated by just watching the thousands of faces on the stands who were cheering the crazy win. That remains my biggest memory from the Camp Nou: it was a victory for our incredible fans. That night, our supporters were our twelfth man. We couldn't have lost in front of them. A few years later, I had the chance to speak to Georghe Hagi, who was the Steaua playmaker, about that final. He confessed to me that his team-mates were scared when they saw how many Milan supporters were there. Someone later said that our win was so easy because Steaua had won their national league the week before and had celebrated too much. I don't know if that was true.

Berlusconi had been our inspiration. He was the first to give us courage to believe that anything is possible. When he arrived, he said that we would soon win the league. When we did, he said the European Cup was the next target. And when we won the World Club Championship a few months later in Tokyo, he wanted us to confirm our dominance the following season. That's why it comes as no surprise that Berlusconi is the most successful President in football history.

Sacchi really was a revolutionary teacher, who made us view the game from a new perspective. The previous coach, Nils Liedholm, wanted us to control games through possession and zonal marking. Sacchi wanted us to play the offside trap and was more interested in our movements off the ball and making the most of the space on the pitch.

Once we left the stadium, we all wanted the same thing: to celebrate with our fans. The Milan board organised a party in the team hotel with our friends and family. Berlusconi was so happy that he sat at the piano and sang a song.

After that, a few of us sneaked out into the streets of Barcelona and went dancing in some clubs. There were huge parties going on and not a Spaniard in sight. Everyone was Italian and even better, from Milan. It was like being at home - except we had the sweet memory from just a few hours earlier, of having raised our European Cup to the skies.

BASILE BOLI
DEFENDER 1990–1994

BORN   2nd January 1967, Adjame, Ivory Coast
SIGNED   1990 from Auxerre
OLYMPIQUE MARSEILLE CAREER   124 games, 20 goals
HONOURS   3 French League titles, 1 Scottish League title,
1 Champions League, 45 France caps
LEFT   Transferred to Glasgow Rangers, 1994; £3m

Basile Boli was a tough centre-back who formed the bedrock of the Marseille defence during their successful period in the early 1990s. Marseille topped the French league in each of his seasons there and were runners-up in the 1991 European Cup final, losing on penalties to Red Star Belgrade. They won the Cup in controversial fashion thanks to Boli's header in 1993. Boli later became a cult hero in Glasgow before ending his career with Urawa Red Diamonds in Japan in 1998. He now works as a TV producer in France and recently set up his own marketing company. He also appears as a pundit on French TV station Canal Plus.

Marseille 1 v AC Milan 0

Wednesday 26 May 1993

Olympiastadion, Munich
Attendance 64,444

Marseille become the first French team to win the European Cup, in the first year of the new Champions League format. Their success comes the third time a French side reaches the final, after Reims lost in 1956 and Saint-Etienne in 1976

Teams

Fabien Barthez	1	Sebastiano Rossi
Jocelyn Angloma	2	Mauro Tassotti
(sub. Jean-Philippe Durand)		
Eric Di Meco	3	Paolo Maldini
Basile Boli	4	Demetrio Albertini
Franck Sauzee	5	Alessandro Costacurta
Marcel Desailly	6	Franco Baresi
Jean-Jacques Eydelie	7	Gianluigi Lentini
Alen Boksic	8	Frank Rijkaard
Rudi Völler	9	Marco Van Basten
(sub. Olivier Thomas)		(sub. Stéfano Eranio)
Abedi Pele	10	Roberto Donadoni
		(sub. Jean-Pierre Papin)
Didier Deschamps	11	Daniele Massaro

Boli 44   **Scorers**

Referee: Rothlisberger (Switzerland)

One of the greatest things about having scored the winning goal in the European Cup final is that nobody can ever take it away from you. It's there in the record books: you have marked history and someone somewhere will always remember you.

That goal I scored follows me around even today. It has become part of me. Remember, Marseille are still the only French team ever to have won the Champions League, and it was my goal that brought them the title. It's a goal that has so much importance, not just for me and that Marseille team, but as it helped show that French football could be successful. For years, we had flattered to deceive. Who would have thought when the European Cup was invented in 1955 that it would take so long for a French side to lift the trophy? There were times when French teams should have done better, but we couldn't win it.

I believe my goal was one that helped inspire other French teams. Paris Saint-Germain went on to win the European Cup Winners' Cup, and maybe it also helped our international side. After that final, many of our team went on to play at top clubs around Europe, where we all learned new skills and different attitudes. Of course just five years later, France won the World Cup.

I was 23 when I went to Marseille. It was Bernard Tapie who signed me. He was starting out on his quest to dominate French football. Tapie was a one-off, there's never been anyone like him in football before or since. He had an amazing energy about him, and at end of the 1980s he set about building one of best teams French football has ever seen.

There was a director of football at Marseille, Jean-Pierre Bernes, but in reality it was Tapie who took all the decisions, from recruitment to picking the team. When he wanted to sign a player, he would call up half a dozen different coaches to ask them for their thoughts. He would be on the phone to every coach in the French First Division every week sounding out their opinion. I know he called people like Arséne Wenger and Rolland Courbis before he signed me. That's how he operated. He'd get the best advice from the best people. He'd say, "What do you think of Boli? I'm thinking of signing him, how do you rate him?"

I was used to working with an eccentric character as my boss because before then I had been at Auxerre from when I was 15. Guy Roux was our coach and it was an extraordinary era. There was a great generation of players who all came through together. I was there at the same time as Eric Cantona, William Prunier,

Bruno Martini, Pascal Vahirua, and Jean-Marc Ferreri, and we all went on to play for France. They were remarkable times. Roux was the boss, he was the man who held the stick and he knew how to use it too.

We were basically apprentices at the club and we lived at the training-centre. Because we were young, we had curfews but I'd often hop over the wall and go into town. I used to nip out and jump on a moped. For the older players, Auxerre is only 90 minutes from Paris, so for a night out they simply drove down the motorway and would get back for training the next day. But Roux had informers all over the town. He knew everyone, including all the employees of motorway toll-booths: they would tell him if any of his players had driven past them.

It was the same for me. If I went anywhere in town, I was bound to be seen by someone who would get word back. One day, Roux found out that I'd been going over the wall and so he padlocked my moped to a lamp-post. A reporter found out about it and the story became big news. The TV stations and the newspapers were reporting on my bike and eventually the news got back to my home in Ivory Coast. The club was inundated with letters and postcards saying, 'Free Basile's Moped' and 'Release the Bike'.

When I joined Marseille in 1990, Marseille had just started dominating French football. By the 1993 Champions League final, we had also become a major power in Europe. We reached the 1991 European Cup final, but lost on penalties to Red Star Belgrade. We should have won that game, we were huge favourites and had a fantastic team. Tapie changed the team every season: in 1991 we had Chris Waddle, Manuel Amoros, Carlos Mozer, and Bernard Casoni. We should have been European champions.

Somehow we managed not to win that year. The following season our team was probably even better, maybe the best we ever had at Marseille: Eric Cantona was still there, as was Waddle, Abedi Pele, Jean-Pierre Papin and Trevor Steven had been signed and was a fantastic recruit. Fabien Barthez was starting out in goal and us guys at the back were rock solid. But we lost in the second round of the European Cup, on away goals to Sparta Prague, that season.

Our coach was Raymond Goethals. He was a very smart guy and a very smart coach. Tapie would bluster into the dressing-room and name the team and say who was doing what. Goethals would stand back, let him give his spiel, wait for Tapie to go, and then give his own team-talk. He'd often begin by saying: "Okay guys, and now I'll tell you really what to do," or another phrase like that. They were like chalk and cheese, those two. Tapie would come into the changing-room like a whirlwind, shouting and yelling at us. Goethals would always be the one to calm us down, and he was a tactical king. He always knew everything about the opposition, he could tell you how each of their players would perform and how the other team could play. He was the master at organising our team to frustrate opponents. He always got the best out of his players and always had us playing to our strengths. We played very high up because we liked to press the opposition and we were very fast at the back. That was our game. We had loads of skilful players too, who could rip teams apart: in my five years at Marseille, I played alongside the likes of Enzo Francescoli, Waddle, Cantona, Dragan Stojkovic, Papin, Abedi Pele, Alen Boksic, and Rudi Völler: what a list of great forwards. And there were some pretty good guys at the back too.

Goethals had an extraordinary football mind: he just seemed to know everything there was to know. He put great trust in his players and he rarely changed his first team. So if you weren't in the team, you probably weren't so keen on him. I know that Cantona never took to him because Goethals had a scheme of play that didn't always involve him. They fell out and it's funny when you look back: maybe Eric should thank Goethals for not picking him regularly. Who knows, he might never had the career he enjoyed so much in England had Goethals found a different way of playing which involved him more.

It was the first year of the new Champions League format, so after our preliminary rounds against Glentoran, which we won 8-0 on aggregate (and I scored one of the goals), we beat Dinamo Bucharest in the quarter-finals and were drawn in a group with Rangers, CSKA Moscow and Club Bruges. Whoever topped the group basically qualified for the final. I remember our first game was against Rangers at Ibrox. We went 2-0 up and thought we had the win wrapped up. But that was without counting for the Rangers fans. They made such a hullabaloo, such a huge wall of noise, that Rangers were spurred on and came back to draw 2-2. In those days we were not the sort of team to let teams recover from 2-0 down. I still get goose-bumps just thinking about the atmosphere in the stadium. That was the night that convinced me to join Rangers.

We beat Bruges and CSKA comfortably at home - we won 6-0 against the Russians - and drew our second match with Rangers. That left us needing to win in Bruges to top the group and qualify for the final. We did that, thanks to an early goal from Alen Boksic.

So we were now in the final, but it was touch and go for several days whether I would be able to play or not. I had a knee problem and it was giving me a lot of trouble. I hadn't been able to play in the now infamous game with Valenciennes. That was the game that cost Marseille their French title that season: it was four days before the Champions League final and Tapie was found guilty of paying off some of the opposing players to go easy in the game. We won it 1-0 anyway and finished top of the league, but later had the title taken away from us as a result of the findings.

Despite all the things he's obviously done wrong, Tapie was an amazing man. He had this capacity to motivate players. He used to always tell Marcel Desailly, who was still young at that time, that he was the best right-back in the world. And he would believe it. Tapie could do that to you. Don't forget, over those years he put together perhaps the best teams that any French club has ever had. We had an incredible spell of success and we had an incredible list of great players pass through the club. Tapie was the man getting those guys in and then getting them out again. The downside was his impulsive side: thankfully I've never seen any other Presidents come charging into the dressing-room at half-time to scream at all the players and tell us we were crap. David Murray certainly never did that when I was at Rangers. But in his defence, Tapie loved football and I'm sure he still does. It was his passion that drove the club on.

So for me, the whole of the build-up to the final against AC Milan was dominated by the 'Would I or wouldn't I be fit to play?' debate. It was horrible. I wouldn't wish it on anyone else. I was so anxious all the time. Plus, from those who had been in the 1991 final, only Eric di Meco and myself were left, so it was important that I was fit for the game.

For the final we stayed at a hotel in Munich that the German national team often used. What really helped more than anything else was the fact that Chris Waddle came to see us before the game. Chris had become my best mate, and we got on really great. We still see each other regularly now and go to games together, and we know each other's families. We even made a record together, called *We've Got a Feeling*, for God's sake. And we did a follow-up single which didn't do so well!

Chris had just moved back to England to play for Sheffield Wednesday, so to have him there was great. He really cheered me up, I was so worried, so frustrated at the idea of not being 100 per cent fit. I'd been spending almost all day every day with the physiotherapist. Chris came along with some new albums for me. He had the latest Wet Wet Wet album and a Bon Jovi album that he recommended which songs I had to listen to. He basically put a smile back on my face. Chris also told me, "You've got to play against Milan, this game is too big to miss."

Of course I was fully aware that this was possibly the biggest game of my career. AC Milan had a team of superstars. They were the overwhelming favourites. People thought they were almost unbeatable, and that just added to the pressure on me to make it.

My team-mates didn't know what it was like for me carrying this injury and not knowing whether I would be able to play. It was so important for me and to be in such a state before a game like this was atrocious. Let's face it, when you know you're going be marking Marco van Basten, you would prefer to be 100 per cent fit. They had a team packed with class: they had Frank Rijkaard, Franco Baresi,

Demetrio Albertini, every name from that side was top-class.

But then we had a pretty good side too. As I said, Barthez was a young goalkeeper, but had lots of talent. I was a kind of sweeper, and with Jocelyn Angloma and Marcel Desailly alongside me, they used to call us the Black Guard. We were all pretty tough and then there was Eric di Meco. There was nothing pretty about him, he was just all tough. Di Meco was a guy you wanted on your team. He had the impression he'd kill you as soon as look at you. At the back we were strong, united and vast. In those days, I could give almost anyone a couple of yards and still be confident of catching them.

You couldn't get many harder-working midfielders than Didier Deschamps, Franck Sauzee and Jean-Jacques Eydelie. Sauzee had one of the most powerful shots in the game. Then there was the fantastic skill of Abedi Pele, who could cross the ball like a god and dribble around whole teams. Rudi Völler was one of the classiest centre-forwards of his time and one hell of a goalscorer. He was a typical fox in the box type of striker and then we had the speed and the wiles of Alen Boksic.

When we got to the final against Milan, we had Papin lining up against us. It was really strange to see him in the opposing colours. For so long he had been one of our main men and one of our best friends. Suddenly he was lining up with the enemy. There he was now with a Milan shirt on and two years earlier he'd been one of our most important players when we knocked them out on the way to the final. I knew that JPP was going be extra-motivated, and totally up for the game. He had so much to prove. No-one wanted to beat us as much as he did, even though in a funny way, it would be heartbreaking for him: he had been such a cult hero at Marseille, he was leading scorer every season he was there. My job was to stop him. He came on as a substitute just after half-time and I went up to him straightaway and said: "If you do anything, you're dead."

It was a tough match, despite the fact there were so many skilful players on the pitch. For a time it seemed like each team was trying to kick the other off the park. There was no love lost. But we were never going to lose out on that front. We had some real men in our team.

They were winding us up. Baresi was dishing out a lot of stick, and I remember he committed a particularly nasty foul on Boksic. I was considered the hard man of our team, the lynchpin at the back and it was my job to respond, like with like. They were getting up my nose. It was important to show them that we would stand up to them. So I responded to Baresi's consistent fouling by giving Van Basten a bit of a knock.

Sadly, I hit him on the ankle that he'd been having problems with. My challenge wasn't an especially nasty one, it was just a bit of tit-for-tat. I got a yellow card, but it wasn't one of those incidents that commentators would have dwelled on. The terrible thing is, it was basically the straw that broke the camel's back. It ended up being the blow that ended his career. That final was the last game he ever played in. It's a terrible thing to have to live with. It could have happened in any other game or at any other time: Marco had problems with that ankle, but I'll always think that it was me that put an end to his great career. That is a source of sadness for me.

Those first 20 minutes were really tough. They made it really hard for us. They were pushing us back, knocking us off our stride. I remember that Fabien made two or three great stops to keep us in the game. That was crucial because it gave us all confidence. The longer we resisted, the more our confidence grew.

Twenty minutes into the game, my knee was killing me and I just wanted to go off. I felt like I wasn't giving of my best and I didn't want to let anybody down. I was in pain. The physio came on and said, "There's no way you're going off. Tapie doesn't want you to."

Rudi came up to me as well and said, "Basile, you can't go off. What am I going do without you?"

I was Rudi's translator in the team. He didn't speak French, he spoke English. Looking back, I guess it's a good thing that I listened to them. And then, just before half-time, there was that corner. It was a fateful corner and I believe replays have since shown it shouldn't even have been given.

It's funny because usually for corners I go to the far post as a matter of course, but something made me change my run and I ended up cutting across Rijkaard and getting to the ball first. I was always renowned for my heading of the ball. I once scored a famous goal in the French league against Paris Saint-Germain, our number one enemies, which people say was actually a header from outside the penalty area. It was said that I could head the ball as powerfully as some people could shoot it.

Rijkaard recently told me a funny story. I was playing for France against Holland and we had a corner. Rijkaard told me that Ronald Koeman was supposed to be marking me, but that he said to Rijkaard, "There's no way I'm going to mark him, he's as big as a gorilla and he's built like a brick wall." And so Van Basten ended up marking me.

Anyway, Abedi Pele swung in the corner and I ran across Rijkaard, made good contact, and the ball flew in. I just went mad. It was only a minute before half-time and we were 1-0 up. Still, we had another 45 minutes to play. I can't really remember much about that second half other than that they were the longest 45 minutes of my life.

I had cried after we lost the final in 1991. Everybody remembered my tears that day. So when we won it two years later, I made a big thing of going up to the

TV cameras and showing my eyes at the end of the game. I made a sign to say that there would be no more crying. If anything, there would only be tears of joy.

When we got back to Marseille after the game, it was absolute mayhem. It was crazy. I don't think anyone has seen anything like it. So many people had come to see us arrive at the airport it was breathtaking. It normally takes about 20 minutes to drive from the airport to the Stade Velodrome, where we knew the ground would be packed with fans to greet us. That day though, after we arrived back at Marseille airport, it took us seven hours to reach the stadium. It was one of the most incredible things I've ever seen.

It's true that I will probably always be remembered for scoring that goal. Wherever I go people still talk to me about it, and nowhere more so than in Marseille where to this day I still have a house. I feel a great attachment to the club and the city. When I go there, I can't go anywhere without the locals wanting to buy me food or drink. I could probably live for the rest of my life in Marseille and never have to pay for anything ever again.

JESPER BLOMQVIST
MIDFIELDER 1998–2001

BORN   5th February 1974, Umeå, Sweden
SIGNED   From Parma, 1998; £4.4m
MANCHESTER UNITED CAREER   38 games, 1 goal
HONOURS   5 Swedish League titles, 1 English League title, 1 FA Cup,
1 Champions League, 30 Sweden caps
LEFT   Transferred to Everton, November 2001

Blomqvist burst onto the scene as a pacy winger whose IFK Gothenburg side
destroyed Manchester United on their way to the 1995 Champions League
quarter-finals. United wanted to buy him then, but he signed for AC Milan
and then Parma before moving to Old Trafford in summer 1998. His first
season was his best, as he played 38 games in United's treble-winning season.
The Champions League final was his last game for United as injuries stalled
his career. He is currently studying to be a coach and working as a pundit on
Swedish TV station TV4.

Manchester United 2 v Bayern Munich 1

Wednesday 26 May 1999

Camp Nou, Barcelona
Attendance 90,000

Manchester United win the title for the first time since 1968 after two late goals cap an astonishing comeback against Bayern

Teams

Peter Schmeichel	Oliver Kahn
Gary Neville	Markus Babbel
Denis Irwin	Thomas Linke
Jaap Stam	Samuel Kuffour
Ronny Johnsen	Michael Tarnat
Nicky Butt	Stefan Effenberg
David Beckham	Lothar Matthäus
	(sub. Thorsten Fink)
Dwight Yorke	Jens Jeremies
Andy Cole	Carsten Jancker
(sub. Ole Gunnar Solskjaer)	
Jesper Blomqvist	Alexander Zickler
(sub. Teddy Sheringham)	(sub. Mehmet Scholl)
Ryan Giggs	Mario Basler
	(sub. Hasan Salihamidzic)

Sheringham 91, Solskjaer 92   **Scorers**   Basler 6

Referee: Collina (Italy)

I remember the night before the Champions League final. We had flown to Spain on Concorde, one of the last ever flights on that plane, and that night we were at our hotel in Barcelona. I was in my room writing a list. "You can do it. You are faster than the rest... You are in good shape..." I was writing things like that to coach myself. I had done it occasionally before, to get myself in the right frame of mind for a game, to get the positive emotions coming. That night, the list was longer than ever. The truth is, I was nervous. I always think it is good to be a little tense, but this time I was too nervous for my own good.

Alex Ferguson had told me two weeks before the final that I was playing. We knew early on that both Roy Keane and Paul Scholes were unavailable for the game. It meant Ryan Giggs moved to the right wing, David Beckham and Nicky Butt were to play in central midfield, and I was to take care of the left wing.

This meant that I had a lot of time to prepare. But the thing is, my confidence wasn't that high. I had played in most of United's away games in the Champions League, but I hadn't played recently in the Premier League, and I didn't play in the FA Cup final. I had also had - as usual - niggling injuries which meant my form wasn't that good, so I was writing this list to convince myself that I would have a good game.

Earlier, when I played for IFK Gothenburg in the Champions League, I never had these kinds of thoughts. Back then, in 1994 and 1996, when we beat Manchester United, Barcelona and AC Milan, everything was just automatic for me. I was young. I didn't know what failure was. I was full of confidence. Now, because I had injuries and too much respect for team-mates as well as the opposition, I was thinking too much.

I usually never had a hard time sleeping, but that night I tossed and turned. I knew it was going to be the biggest game of my career, and it was very frustrating not to feel great about it.

I had written a similar list to myself at the beginning of the season, at another hotel. Then, I was questioning my move to Manchester United. I must be one of very few players who wasn't over the moon about going to United. As much as I learned to love the club, I was worried about my own decision. When I left IFK in 1996 I could pick any club. All the big teams wanted me: Milan, Manchester United, Barcelona. I was so stubborn that I never listened to any advice. I wanted to go to Milan, and that was it. It was my boyhood dream.

I talked to Sven-Göran Eriksson, who wanted me to come to Sampdoria. I talked to Jonas Thern, who was captain of the national team and played for Roma, and he advised me to go to a smaller club. But my mind was set: I wanted Milan. My career path was on a fast rise upwards, and I had no doubts about my ability. I guess I didn't realise - or didn't want to realise - what a big step it was, going from small and cosy IFK to one of the biggest clubs in the world.

I guess I thought I was pretty cool, but when I look back now, I see how inexperienced I really was. I mean, when I walked into that AC Milan dressing-room, wearing my washed-out jeans and white sports socks, I can understand now if they were laughing behind my back. I was so naive, very much a countryside boy from Sweden. I didn't know the language. I hadn't even seen a risotto or knew what a parmesan cheese looked like.

Anyway, for the first season I played in most of the games, either from the start or as a substitute. I adapted to the tactical Italian game. But still, I knew very little Italian. The players minded their own business, it was very different from the team spirit I was used to at IFK. Milan had their worst season in ages, and the dressing-room was silent. Paolo Maldini and Zvonimir Boban were two of the players who spoke English, so they helped me out a bit. They taught me some of the mentality that creates a successful professional.

I have been brought up not to boast, not to believe that you are better than anyone else. Then one day, I was talking to Boban about tennis, as he was very into the game.

He asked me, "Are you any good at tennis?"

"Well, I'm okay," I answered.

Then he said, "Okay? Well, I guess there is no point in us playing then, because I am damn good."

He may well have been better than me, but even if I had won Wimbledon, I would still probably have said, "I'm okay." It was a clash of mentalities, and I had to learn to take other people's confidence into consideration. I still try to learn from it, although I'm pretty much the same as I used to be.

After six months Andreas Andersson, my former team-mate from IFK, joined Milan. I thought that was great, and I was confident things would be better socially from then on. In a way they were, but hanging out with Andreas all the time meant there was even less interaction with the rest of the team. Andreas ended up having me as his guide to Italy, and I don't think he learned many words in Italian during his time there. After he arrived, there was not only one but two Swedish bodies who didn't quite belong at Milanello.

Things got worse for me on the pitch too. The coach Arrigo Sacchi, who saw something in me and gave me confidence, quit because of poor results. Fabio Capello came in, and a few weeks into the 1997-98 season, we had a talk.

"You are my fifth or sixth choice on left midfield," he said.

My first instinct was to continue fighting and prove him wrong, but then I thought, 'If he doesn't have confidence in me, why should I stay?' It would be a long, uphill battle.

I knew Parma were interested, and a transfer was agreed within a week. Capello then almost spoiled it when he said, "Jesper, you can't go: you are my second choice on the left wing."

I was so angry with him. I told him I couldn't work under these conditions and I wanted to leave as soon as possible. In retrospect, I took it much too personally, which I had a tendency to do. But I was so disappointed with him. Anyway, I moved to Parma in October 1998.

A few weeks after I joined Parma, we met Milan in the Italian Cup. We won 3-1. It was one of the best matches I have ever played. I was named Man of the Match, and it was just because I was so angry with Capello. I was so fired up. Capello wasn't too happy after the game, and he said a few harsh words to me in the tunnel afterwards. But it only made me feel better.

Life was easier at Parma. It was a smaller club, a smaller town and the expectations of the team were lower. It suited me, and I had a very good year. I felt that I had found my feet in Italy. I had found a club who wanted me, and I enjoyed working with the coach, Carlo Ancelotti.

That's why I was so bewildered when Alex Ferguson came in for me. Everything went so fast. One week I was preparing for a new season with Parma, the next I was at a hotel in Manchester. The other day, by chance, I found the notebook from that first night in Manchester. I had written: "How did this happen? Do I really want to be here? I didn't want to leave Parma, and I didn't want to leave Italy. How will this end? How can I find my joy in football again?"

I guess no other player would have been so down after signing with United. That diary entry ended, "I will survive this period like the others."

It wasn't as bad as it might sound. After all, I knew that Ferguson had watched me for several years, and he really wanted me to be a part of his United team. I had played well for IFK when we beat United in 1994. In fact, the games against Barcelona and Manchester United in 1994 were really important for my career. I had started for Sweden in the World Cup that summer, but I only had 15 games for IFK under my belt. I wasn't ready for something as big as the World Cup, even if I didn't realise it then. Instead the Champions League games with IFK, where I felt more comfortable than in the national team, were great for me. It was a good opportunity for us. We knew we had a good team and believed that we could beat anyone, especially at home.

At the same time, teams like Barcelona and Manchester United probably under-estimated us. Once they realised that we were tough opposition, it was mentally too late for them to switch. When we had played United, David May was at right-back for them and I was playing like I was in a trance. Everything worked for me. I scored one goal, and won a penalty for our third as we came out 3-1 winners. I know that Ferguson had followed me closely after that.

We talked a lot before agreeing on the move. I wanted to know how he saw Ryan Giggs and myself as players, and he made it clear that he would try his best to make room for both of us in the team. I wasn't scared of the competition: at Milan I had to compete with Leonardo, Christian Ziege, Boban and Edgar Davids for a place. But Giggs and I were similar as players, and he was a true Manchester United icon.

Ferguson was very supportive and friendly when we had these talks. I almost felt he overdid it - he was carrying my bags at the airport and things like that - but I always felt he was sincere. It didn't stop me thinking I had made the wrong move, though.

The first weeks at a new club are usually exciting, when everything is new. But this time, it was the other way around. Manchester United was a huge club to come to. As a player, you notice it by all the people working there. United have their own carpenter, their own plumber, there are so many people to get to know. I like to know the people I work with, to have some personal relations at the club. This is more difficult if you are with Milan or Manchester United. If you are not someone like Dwight Yorke, who is always laughing, and never had any worries, settling in a big club takes time for everyone. For me, who started off with a foot injury that kept me sidelined and not able to train with my new team-mates for a few weeks, it took three months. Only then, I thought, 'I like this club, things will be good here'.

I got to know the other Scandinavians, and spent a lot of time with Ronny Johnsen, Ole Gunnar Solskjaer, Henning Berg, and Raimond van der Gouw from Holland. That is the way it usually is at clubs: the foreigners stick together. The English already had their friends and families. I think Phil Neville was the one I got to know best of the English players.

The change from Italy to Manchester United was of course not as big as when I first moved to AC Milan. I had made my name, and carried more respect with me when I came to United. Still, there were people on the team who you didn't mess with. Roy Keane was the obvious number one in the hierarchy. It took me a year to understand what he was about. For a long time I just thought he was mad, or annoying. He was always shouting, arguing, criticising and being provocative. I thought he was so selfish and egotistic. But after a while I realised that, even if his methods were strange, he always put the team first.

As a Swede who believes there are other kinds of solutions to problems - and I still think there are better methods than his - I thought he was strange. But everything he did was because of the team.

Some of the guys received a lot of stick: poor Phil Neville, for example, got more than his share. I think Phil is a better footballer than his brother, but he doesn't have Gary's mental strength. But Ferguson let Keane go on, because he saw that his outbursts ultimately benefited the team. I guess that Keane eventually crossed the line of what was acceptable, and that was when he had to leave.

Keane was furious with me after the second leg of the semi-final against Juventus. It was a fantastic game, which started with us going 2-0 down in the first ten minutes. But Keane scored from a header soon after, and Dwight Yorke made it 2-2 before half-time. With five minutes left, Andy Cole completed the comeback: it was a game that gave us so much confidence for the final, and helped us believe that nothing was impossible.

For Keane, though, his tournament ended with that game. I hit a pass to him that was intercepted by one of the Juventus players, and Roy felt he had to make a tackle on Zinedine Zidane to stop him starting a counter-attack. He was yellow-carded, and knew there and then that he would miss the final. I remember his eyes when he looked at me after that tackle.

"It's your fucking fault that I'm going to miss the final," he said.

It was tough to hear, of course, but I didn't care too much. That was the way he worked. Things were never his fault.

I have seen the incident on TV since then. It was a bad pass by me, I admit that, but it was also a bad first touch by Keane. Also, it was in the middle of the pitch, and there were still a lot of players who could have covered that Juventus attack.

He kept talking about it for a few weeks afterwards. Then it turned into a running joke, and he always referred to it during my time at Old Trafford. I can understand it in a way. The game we had just qualified for was the biggest game of our careers.

Peter Schmeichel was the other one who dictated things on the pitch. He tried hard to become the number one, but he had to settle for the number two spot in the hierarchy. I remember once at training, Schmeichel and I clashed when chasing a loose ball. I went in hard and tackled him, and he was furious. He took a swipe at me and was very close to starting a real fight, which wouldn't have been good. He was twice as big as me. I would have been crushed.

I told him I thought he was crazy and a fool, and that I wouldn't accept the way he was treating me.

"I won't speak to you until you change your attitude," I said.

It was a bit childish of me, but it worked. I didn't say a word to him for two weeks and then, after training, he just came up one day, chatting like normal, checking out how things were going. I think I got his respect from then on, and also the respect of other guys in the team who appreciated that I had stood my ground.

I had spells of a few games here and there where I really enjoyed my football at United. Those were the times I felt relaxed and at ease, the way it was when I was younger. We played against Brondby in the group stages and I had that feeling of being invincible. We had already drawn with Barcelona 3-3 and Bayern Munich 2-2, and we went to Denmark and won 6-2 over there. I was playing with confidence and was involved in our goals. Then they came to Old Trafford and we won 5-0.

There were other games when I felt really good, like the time we beat Southampton 3-0 away from home, and West Ham 4-1 at home. We also beat Everton 4-1 away, when I scored my only goal for the club.

United was such a great team to play for. I developed my passing game immensely. Everything we did was based on passing and movement. We had two fantastic forwards in Yorke and Cole: when I look at TV footage now, it is almost surreal how well they combine with each other. We had Scholes, who never worked very hard in training, but was such a big talent. Then there was David Beckham, who was quiet and shy, but a leader on the pitch. He could run forever and took training more seriously than anyone else.

But all my small injuries meant that there was always a setback, always a dip in the curve for me. I was never able to put together a string of matches where I was playing really well to get that extra confidence I needed.

Also, I had changed my playing style to something that was not really me. For United that season, I played in most of the away games in the Champions League. Ferguson saw me as a more defensive player than Ryan Giggs. It was a bit strange, because my game, when I was at my best, was using my speed to beat defenders. In Italy I developed the defensive side of my play, and in a way forgot a little of what made me a good player. I became more cautious, I stopped going at defenders the way I had done at IFK. I had too much respect for everyone: the opponents, my team-mates and coaches.

I definitely wasn't at ease or relaxed before the Champions League final. I was a player who needed to feel the support of my team-mates and my coach. It wasn't that the other players didn't accept me, but they hadn't played with me for three or four games, which meant they were not used to me being in the team.

And I guess I did feel the coach's confidence. After all, he was playing me in the Champions League final. At other times Ferguson's pre-game talk would usually boost everyone's confidence.

When we played against Internazionale in the quarter-final, he said, "Lads, Inter are just a bunch of individual stars. They don't have any team spirit at all. You are so much better then they are." We won that first leg 2-0 at home and drew 1-1 away two weeks later. Paul Scholes scored a late equaliser in the San Siro at the end of a tense game.

Before the Juventus game, Ferguson had said, "Juventus are a hell of a team, but they don't have any star players like we do. Individually, you are much better." And he was talking about a team who started with Alessandro del Piero, Edgar Davids, Zinedine Zidane and Pippo Inzaghi!

By the time we got to the final, against Bayern Munich, he told us: "Munich are good, but nowhere near as good as us. The only way they can score against us is from set-pieces."

He always had a firm belief in his own team, and even if he exaggerated at times, I usually believed all the things he said during his team-talks. He was incredibly good at making his players feel confident. But that day, when I went onto the Camp Nou pitch, I was still nervous.

I remember walking out and seeing all the fans. I tried to remember that I had played well on this ground before, with IFK, and that I could do it again. We had drawn 1-1 when we met Barcelona in the group stages in late-1994, and when we played them at our place, I scored the winner with a header. I had also played in the 3-3 draw for United earlier that season in Barcelona, and done well.

But in the final against Bayern, I was never calm when the ball was at my feet. I rushed things. I passed the ball too quickly. Team-mates can sense this: it doesn't take long to spot if someone in your team is nervous or having a bad day. When you are on form, you instil confidence in your team-mates, and make them more secure. When you are not, the opposite happens.

I never reached the standard I should have in that game. I wasn't particularly bad, but I didn't contribute in the way I would have hoped. I never really threatened the Munich defence. You should remember that we didn't have a very good game as a team. Both our central midfielders, Keane and Scholes, were out, and naturally we missed them. I remember the feeling of not being sharp. My form on the day wasn't the best, and it is a frustrating feeling, especially when you are playing the Champions League final.

Mario Basler opened the scoring for them after six minutes, but we were lucky not to have conceded more goals. At half-time our spirits were down. None of us seemed to really believe that we could turn it around. But none of us were really upset either. We just tried to gather ourselves together and try harder in the second half.

I had one good chance at the beginning of the second half. I threw myself at a cross from David Beckham, but my shot missed the target. It wasn't a bad miss, because it happened so fast, but if I had got the ball on target, I don't think Oliver Kahn would have saved it. It's a thin line between failure and success. Today, people remember that I had a bad game and was subbed off. But if I had scored then, no-one would have cared that I didn't play too well.

It was maybe ten minutes later when I went off, and Teddy Sheringham came on. There was just over 20 minutes left to play. It was a disappointment to be substituted, but at the time it felt natural.

I sat there on the bench, watching the clock tick away. I thought of games when I have played well, and wondered why this hadn't been one of those times. The mood on the bench was low. We knew we only needed one goal, one lucky kick, but to be honest we hadn't created much.

Then it happened so quickly, with the goals from Sheringham and then Solskjaer, that there hardly was any time to react in between. There was euphoria, the feeling that something impossible had just happened. Everyone was just dancing and hugging. I realised immediately that this was something I would never have a chance to repeat in my career. I mean, playing for a club like United, and winning three trophies in one season. And the way it happened. I was so happy: for the club, the fans and the players who had been at United for so long.

The contrasts were unbelievable. The Bayern players were crying. Sammy Kuffour was so upset, he beat the ground in frustration. Lothar Matthäus just looked blank. Four years earlier, it had been the other way round for me: Bayern had beaten IFK on away goals in the quarter-finals of the competition. It was a sweet revenge for me.

But the strangest feeling was my own. I was proud and happy. Yet I still felt that I hadn't contributed.

I was always thinking too much, at least after I left IFK. Some players can easily forget a bad pass or a bad game, and get on with life. I couldn't help thinking that I could have played a bigger part, made a bigger impact. If I compare it to the games when I was IFK, when we had good results in the Champions League, I felt better then, as I was one of the main players in the team.

Now, I was part of something historic, but my biggest achievement had been to leave the field to make room for Sheringham, who scored a goal. It was a strange feeling.

As it happened, it turned out to be more or less my last game for United. My knees started breaking up into pieces, and I was left to train in the gym and on the bike. It makes me sad to think about it. After my three years there, when I left the club I was finally in tune with it. I knew all the people, the players, and understood how things worked there.

By then, I had stayed there longer than I could have asked for. Ferguson even let me train with the team and play for the reserves in 2001. I would have loved to have a second chance there, to show the fans what I could do. But when I was healthy, I wasn't mentally ready to play a big part at United. When my mind was there, my knees were gone. If I was with United now, I would have had a healthier distance from what I was doing. I wouldn't be Dwight Yorke, but I would take things a bit easier. I was over-serious for many of the years when I played, and took people's comments or my own difficulties too much to heart.

Looking back, I don't have any regrets now about joining United. My time there gave me memories that I will keep with me for as long as I live. I still have a replica of all three trophies we won that season - the Premier League, the FA Cup and the Champions League - on my mantelpiece.

Many people questioned my decision to go to United because of Ryan Giggs. But I have to say that Ferguson kept his word. He really tried to fit us both into the team. Giggs and I both had a lot of injuries during my time at United. Either he was playing and I was out, or it was the other way around. When we both were fit and in shape I always played on the left wing.

I always felt that Ferguson liked me. He was temperamental, of course, and when he was yelling in the dressing-room everyone was quiet as schoolboys. I received the hair-dryer treatment once. I don't remember what he thought I had done wrong, maybe he just wanted to shout at someone. I just sat there, trying to ride out the storm.

But Ferguson helped me a lot during the periods I was injured. He recommended me to other clubs, he let me practice with the team for six months, and play with the reserves when I was out of contract. He was never friendly to journalists, obviously, but at Old Trafford or at the training-ground, he used to walk around singing or humming.

Eventually I went to Everton, on a free transfer, in 2001. One of my career highs was when I was able to play again at Goodison Park for Everton without feeling any pain in my knees. I had a number of games when I was in really good shape, including once when I played against Manchester United, which was a magical moment. It was like all the hard work in the gym had finally paid off.

Everton was very different to United. Everything was more family-like and the atmosphere was more good-humoured. I also liked David Moyes as a coach. He was hard, tough, organised and had clear ideas about the way he wanted to play. He was good at communicating this to the players.

Still, when the new season came, he couldn't guarantee me anything in terms of playing time, and I knew that it was time to go. I was close to joining Middlesbrough and Steve McClaren, who knew me from Manchester United, but then I had another knee injury, and he got cold feet.

Instead I went to Charlton, which turned out to be a disaster for me and the club. My knees never healed, and I travelled back and forth between England and Sweden, and England and Croatia, where I had doctors who I trusted. I was so stubborn, I didn't want to use the knee experts that the club suggested, but only the ones I knew from before.

As a last effort to salvage something from my career, I signed a contract with Djurgården, in Sweden's top division, the Allsvenskan. I played 13 games and scored one goal, but was only playing at 70 per cent of my capacity. Now I am trying to find something else to do. I have done some TV commentating and I am studying leadership and coaching at university, as part of my training to become a football coach.

I still have a hard time watching football. There are so many players that I know who are still playing, and it hurts that I am not one of them. I see Teddy Sheringham play in the Premiership. I hear that Dwight Yorke and Niclas Alexandersson, who I played with at IFK and Everton, are preparing for the World Cup in Germany. The other day I met up with Ronny Johnsen in Stockholm. He was here playing with Valerenga, his Norwegian club. All these guys are older than I am, and it makes me think that I could have been there too.

At least the memories of the Champions League win are sweeter today. I started realising that I should be proud of what I had achieved at the home-coming after the final. When we travelled through Manchester in that open double-decker bus, and saw all the people celebrating, I knew that I had been part of a chapter in history. We had a reception at the Manchester Arena after our return from Barcelona. And the feeling of lifting the trophy in the Manchester Arena, and hearing the cheers of nearly 20,000 fans bounce off the walls, that is probably the best memory of my career.

IKER CASILLAS
GOALKEEPER 1997–PRESENT

BORN   20th May 1981, San Sebastian, Spain
SIGNED   1997 as Apprentice
REAL MADRID CAREER*   295 games
HONOURS*   2 Spanish League titles, 2 Champions Leagues,
1 Intercontinental Cuo, 1 European Super Cup, 53 Spain caps
*Up to and including 1 March 2006

Iker Casillas started playing for Real Madrid youth teams aged eight and when he broke into the first team 11 years later, he still used public transport to get to training. His ended his first season at the club playing in the 2000 Champions League final and was soon selected for Spain. He temporarily lost his place at Real in the 2001-02 season, but since starring as a substitute in the 2002 Champions League final, has remained Real Madrid's number one. He is now established first-choice for club and country and is widely recognised as one of the best goalkeepers in the world.

Real Madrid 2 v Bayer Leverkusen 1

Wednesday 15 May 2002

Hampden Park
Attendance 51,456

Real Madrid win their third Champions League final in five years

Teams

César Sánchez	Hans-Jörg Butt
(sub. Iker Casillas)	
Míchel Salgado	Zoltan Sebescen
	(sub. Ulf Kirsten)
Roberto Carlos	Boris Zivkovic
Fernando Hierro	Lucio
	(sub. Marko Babic)
Iván Helguera	Diego Placente
Luis Figo	Bernd Schneider
(sub. Steve McManaman)	
Claude Makelele	Carsten Ramelow
(sub. Flavio Conceiçao)	
Zinedine Zidane	Yildiray Basturk
Santigao Solari	Michael Ballack
Raul	Oliver Neuville
Fernando Morientes	Thomas Brdaric
	(sub. Dimitar Berbatov)

Raul 8, Zidane 44   Scorers   Lucio 14

Referee: Meier (Switzerland)

There were just over 20 minutes left when César Sanchez got injured and I realised I was going to go on for the remainder of the 2002 Champions League final against Bayer Leverkusen in Glasgow. It came out of the blue for me: if anyone doubted that I wasn't expecting to play, they could see that I wasn't ready, right down to me still having to cut the sleeves off my goalkeeper's shirt.

Suddenly, everything was a panic. Where are the scissors? Cut the sleeves off, quick! I always played with short sleeves and as far as I was concerned, it genuinely mattered. It wasn't a question of superstition or some lucky charm, it was just what I always did. I'm far more comfortable in short sleeves. I would always cut the sleeves off before matches normally and no-one would even notice a kerfuffle, but I wasn't going to play so I hadn't bothered cutting them off before the final. Besides, it was cold in Glasgow! I wasn't going to sit there on the bench freezing in short sleeves, was I?

When César got injured the first thing I did was search for some scissors and cut the sleeves off, grab my gloves, and sort out the tape around my wrists. A goalkeeper's preparation takes far longer than that of an outfield player and all that rushing about became the image of the final for me - especially the sleeves. Lots of people have asked me about it since. I could have had the sleeves already cut underneath my tracksuit top, but I really didn't think I was going to play. How often does a goalkeeper get injured in a match, let alone a Champions League final? I learnt my lesson, though: that was the moment that I starting getting my shirts made with short sleeves. No more scissors.

When César came past me, he didn't say anything. He was so angry at having to go off. He was wound up, deeply disappointed and just left the field silently. I understood that: he was playing in an important final, the biggest club game there is, and he had got injured. Of course he was annoyed. When I went on, the only thing I was thinking was how grateful I was to be getting the opportunity to play in a Champions League final because I didn't expect to get the chance.

Going on because a team-mate has suffered an injury is not the nicest way to get a chance, but I was happy to form a little part of Real Madrid's history. Naturally, there is a selfish bit of you that is delighted. For me, just playing was the important thing. I wasn't thinking about how the game might go or about being European champion - and I certainly wasn't thinking, "I can be the hero here." I couldn't believe I was going on, but it felt like I deserved it.

If you are playing in the starting XI, you have to believe it's because you have earned it in training. Likewise, if you lose your place you have to accept that the guy who takes your place has earned it. But that does not mean it hurt any less. I had been playing for three seasons in the starting XI and then over the last couple of months I'd suddenly lost my place in the team to César. I respected coach Vicente del Bosque's decision, but I thought I was worthy of a place in the side and privately I was angry. There was a sense of making up for all that lost time when I ran on. I had played in the league and we had stayed neck-and-neck with Valencia; I had played in the Champions League up until the quarter-finals; and I had helped take the team to the final of the Copa del Rey. So as far as I was concerned, I was playing well and still deserved a place. I couldn't understand why I was dropped. Now, I had the chance to make up for it.

And yet, when I went on the pitch, I wasn't thinking, "I'll show them." I was just thankful for the chance. I was thinking how fantastic it was to have the chance to play in another final and that I could help Real Madrid win a ninth European Cup, which is the trophy that most obsesses Madrid fans, the one that really defines the club.

It was a difficult time to come on. We were 2-1 up, thanks to goals from Raúl and that stunning volley from Zinedine Zidane, but we were struggling. We were under a lot of pressure and it seemed like if anyone was going to score it was them. The fact that it was so hard seems to have surprised people, but it didn't surprise me in the slightest.

Bayer Leverkusen were a good team, a properly good team. They might have been playing in their first final and were not the most famous club in the tournament, but I thought they were an excellent side, with some exceptional players. They had got through the competition playing great football and defeating a lot of good teams. I remember in the semi-finals they knocked out Manchester United, who were consistently going far in the competition at the time, and they had also knocked out Liverpool. So I was under no illusions, even if some people were.

Besides, it's always difficult in a final, whoever you are playing. We were favourites because of our name and some of the great players we had, but that was irrelevant as far as I was concerned. You're not going to go out there and win a final 5-0. That just doesn't happen. When we went 2-1 up, they started to push us back. They started to get chances and we just had to defend them as best we could. There was nothing else we could do.

The pressure was intense. We were lost. We didn't know how to stop them and all we could think about was holding them off, desperately trying to keep them out and maybe catching a goal on the break. Although we were winning, we knew that we would have to suffer if we were to win it and that is exactly what happened.

For me, personally, of course, that helped to make it a special final. I made a few saves as they put us under pressure. One in particular came when Dimitar Berbatov shot from only about two metres away, but I just managed to save the ball with my feet. The fans tend to remember Zidane and me as the heroes: him for the goal and me for the saves. But I still maintain that there was a lot of fortune involved. They weren't spectacular saves, they were more ones where you have to be there. It was about speed rather than spectacular stops. But those saves did keep us in the game.

I understand the way the fans went on about my performance and, of course, I was delighted, but the truth is that on a personal level the best was yet to come: after the final, the Valencia goalkeeper Santiago Cañizares got injured when he dropped an aftershave bottle on his foot and severed a tendon. That gave me the chance to go to the World Cup as Spain's number one and that was even bigger for me. I played well in Korea, especially during the penalty shoot-out against Ireland, which we won. I came back a different person and a different player. More than anything else it was those few months, when I went from a substitute in Glasgow to a hero in Korea, that catapulted me to where I am now.

People ask me what the secret is to stopping penalties, but there isn't one: it's luck. When a player starts his run-up, you watch his movement, you think about what kind of footballer he is, how he strikes a ball, which way it's going to go - but so much of it is down to luck. In Korea I was lucky, but that, allied to Glasgow, really helped to make me. Lots of people said I must be the luckiest man alive: first César gets injured in the Champions League final then Cañizares gets injured on the eve of the World Cup. I had a flower, as the Spanish say. Or even a whole bunch of them!

But you have to be able to take advantage. What's the point of getting the opportunity if you then make loads of horrific mistakes? You have to be capable of waiting for your opportunity and making sure you don't waste it when it comes along. The 2002 final was the perfect example. It hurt to be left out, but I kept my mouth shut, carried on working and got the reward in the end.

When you make a save you're not thinking, "Wow, that was a good one!" You're thinking, "Hey, watch it! This lot could score here! This is dangerous! If they score again we're going to extra-time!"

That was definitely the sensation during the final against Bayer Leverkusen. I was so conscious of the fact that they just kept coming back at us. There certainly wasn't any time to glory in making those saves. It was nervy, edgy, worrying stuff. Looking back, that's probably the scariest thing I have been through. The final whistle was a relief.

When the ref blew for full-time, I started crying. Along with the saves, especially the one in the last minute from Yildiray Basturk's shot, when I slid on my knees towards the post, that ended up being the image of me that most sticks in people's heads from the final: that and the sleeves, of course. I left the field crying. So many things came together to provoke those tears. It was a mixture of emotions, there were so many things bundled up in my thoughts and my feelings: anger, sadness, delight, redemption, the works.

I would say that I cried more out of anger and relief than happiness. It was more annoyance, pent-up frustration coming out than anything else. I know we had just won the Champions League, but in some ways I cared more about having gone months without playing. That really hurt me. In the long run it helped me a lot. All's well that ends well, I suppose. I was out for a couple of months and really analysed things. That made me stronger, it gave me more character, both with myself and with others. It's hard when things seem to be going so well and you think everything's fine, then suddenly you're out the team.

I was also crying out of nostalgia, out of the fact that I missed my family. The only members of my family that had made the trip to Glasgow were my dad and my brother. My mother had stayed back in Madrid and quite a lot of my friends hadn't come either because I wasn't playing, so I felt a bit lost and sad that at such an important moment in my career, lots of the people closest to me weren't there. Still, at least they watched on the TV and although I didn't think that was as good as them being there, they really enjoyed it. They found it exciting and emotional too. And it was emotional, the way it worked out. I loved the fact that everyone suffered! That's how football should be.

I spoke to them all after the game, and they were all congratulating me, telling me that I deserved it because of all the work I had put into it. I was happy and so were they. They congratulated me for having kept my mouth shut, for not having complained, for having just got on with things despite the fact I thought I deserved a place in the side.

I was only 20 - I turned 21 a few days later - but I don't consider myself stupid and didn't then either: you see that you've been playing well and you know that you're good enough to play in the final. I wasn't playing badly in any competition and that plays with your head in the sense that you think to yourself, "What's going on here?"

On the inside, I knew I was capable of playing and I felt like I should be playing. My tears were tears of anger, but I try not to think about it too much. It's done now, that's the way it went and it's all over. The moment that I got the chance to go onto the pitch everything changed and I can't complain because it turned out right.

I may have been just 20 years-old, but it was already my second Champions League final. I was very young. I'd won my first Champions League at 18, but it never really fazed me. These days, if I think about an 18-year-old kid playing in the Real Madrid first-team, it strikes me as totally insane but the thing is, I did it. Now I realise what that meant and I'm able to value it and judge it for what it is far more than I did at the time. When I see kids come up to the first-team now, I think to myself, "Let's see how he copes with this." But at the time I didn't think of it like that. It just seemed so right.

After the final, the dressing-room was madness. In fact, it was like that after both finals. After we won the club's eighth European Cup by beating Valencia 3-0 in Paris, it was much the same as it was after Glasgow. Whenever you secure a big victory, dressing-rooms are special. It's there more than anywhere else that you really enjoy it, especially if we're talking about a Champions League final. You basically get the freedom to behave a bit ridiculously. Glasgow was totally ridiculous. When you see the photos and videos you think, "Did I really do that? What a fool!"

But at the time it's great. You love it because it is a moment of sheer happiness where frankly you deserve to go mad for a bit. That's when you can really let your hair down, there's such a release. There are photos of me pulling faces, messing about, jumping up and down, going crazy, screaming and shouting. You're so happy that anything goes at that stage.

When we won the tournament in Paris we had a huge meal in the city and then flew back to Madrid to celebrate with the fans at Cibeles, the fountain in the city centre where the supporters gather to mark all the club's successes - a tradition which I understand took root with the club's first European victories. We clambered all over it and just went mad. It was great to be able to share that emotion and joy with the supporters. In Glasgow, it was much the same, but the celebrations didn't last so long. There were parties back in Madrid, and then almost straight after it was off to the World Cup. My brother and dad were there in Glasgow and we were hanging around with some of the other players' families and it was a great laugh.

I also watched the game again, of course. I know Zinedine watched it over and over that night and, while I didn't go so far, I have seen it on video loads of times since. When you watch it again you appreciate how special it was, how exciting. So many factors came together to make it special: a goalkeeper getting injured, which doesn't exactly happen often in the Champions League final, the saves, the fact that it came after a really tough period when I lost my place, the fact that it hurtled me towards the World Cup, the fact that I was still so young, that it was our second Champions League in three years. With time, that becomes even more special because we haven't won the tournament again since.

When you watch the video again, it all comes back and you can digest it all a bit better. Hopefully, one day my kids can watch it and enjoy it. It's a good job there are subs these days, unlike back in the era when the club first won the European Cup with Alfredo Di Stéfano, Ferenc Puskás, Paco Gento. If not, César would have had to carry on or we'd have been forced to put an outfield player in goal. I would never have got the chance. Afterwards, you watch it and watch it, and you feel a swell of pride at having formed part of the history of the Champions League and of the club.

We were playing very well, but I don't think we were thinking that we would go on and win it the next year. Sure, we were confident, but even then, amidst the euphoria, you know that it's very difficult to win it the following year. You have to know how to take advantage of the success, enjoy it, and live it to the maximum. You don't know when you're going to get another chance. Madrid went 32 years without winning it and we got to three finals in five years. And we won them all.

People have wondered why we didn't go on and win more, especially as that was the only final when we had more than one *galáctico* in the team: Luis Figo and Zinedine Zidane. In theory, we had a better side, in terms of names, in future years, with the arrival of the other superstars, but we were unable to replicate the success of 2000 and 2002. However, I think the reality is that we did have great players in 2000 and 2002: and the team had that little extra something special too. People haven't really done justice to those teams. Or, indeed, to the team that won the club's seventh European Cup against Juventus in Amsterdam in 1998.

The *galácticos* is a nickname that the press has pinned on us. Originally it was something that seemed funny, but then they carried on and on and on about it. There was so much talk, the *galáctico* tag stuck and we have been lumbered with it. We don't really worry about it, but far from benefiting from it I think it hasn't done us any favours. In fact, I would say it has done us a lot of damage. I'm not a *galáctico*, I'm just a bloke who has come up from the youth team. End of story.

The Real Madrid team that won the 2000 and 2002 Champions Leagues had something special. Although more famous players arrived later, there were excellent players at the club before the so-called *galáctico* era. Even in terms of names, we had great players and the atmosphere when we won the eighth European Cup was a healthy atmosphere. Almost all of us were Spaniards and there were lots of young guys, all with great hope and dreams, real ambition and drive. When we won the ninth European Cup in Glasgow we had more or less the same team, with the odd addition, like Santiago Solari and Zidane, but then it started slipping away. Other people have joined, but since then we have been unable to win things. We have had bad luck.

Even the people who were not Spanish back then somehow managed to be Spanish in their outlook: Redondo and Roberto Carlos had been in Spain for a long time and were perfectly integrated. It was a very healthy atmosphere. We used to all go out and eat together. It was much more happy, more united, more comfortable.

That was the environment I walked into when I first got into the side. I was very, very young - I made my debut at 17, while I was still at school - but I was lucky enough to be surrounded by lots of young guys. There was Iván Helguera, Míchel Salgado, and Fernando Morientes and when you see that many young people, you feel part of it. You use them as a support base when you first get into the team and that really helps. There were lots of jokers in the team, too. Iván was the worst - and I was one of the ones who most fell for his jokes because I was so young. But that was one of the great things about that team. Cracking jokes and taking the mickey out of people helped unity. It helped everyone get along better. I couldn't really say why it seemed so natural, but we all got on, it all seemed right somehow.

We also had Fernando Hierro, our captain. He was an imposing figure, he carried such weight and played a huge role. He would almost mange the team, both on and off the pitch. He was the one that managed the relationship between the players and the club, with the press, and even with the fans. You could say that lots of us who are here now learnt things, a lot of things, from him. I'm now a veteran in the first-team, having been here for seven years and I have learnt so much from him: I now consider myself to be important in a similar way, in terms of transmitting the meaning and identity of the club onto others.

The club is different for me than it is for the others. I've been here for so long that I don't think my experience of the club, the way I live Real Madrid, is the same. No-one can say that someone who's been at a club for nine years sees that club in the same way as someone who's been here for one season. Even if I haven't been in the first-team all that time, it doesn't matter. It's totally different. I was made here - as a footballer and a person - and I have tried to continue what Fernando did. You understand the identity of the club, so you play a role in terms of listening to players, looking after them, making them feel better about themselves, giving people confidence, explaining what the club is about. That's very important. It was important to have a leader to say things to you when he had to; someone you looked up to and listened to.

All those factors came together and helped to make us European champions. It's a shame that we have been unable to replicate that since and of course the whole *galáctico* thing has put extra pressure on us. But I don't think it's quite that simple. I think it's more a case of the fact that people got too used to us winning things and that was wrong. That really did put pressure on us.

They got used to us wining the League, the Copa del Rey, the Champions League and people began to expect us to win even more, to keep on improving all the time.

They expected us to win everything every season and maybe didn't appreciate how hard that is. Winning the treble - the League, the Cup, and the Champions League - in a single season just doesn't happen. Manchester United have done it once and maybe a few other teams have done it, but that is what people began expecting from us.

They didn't seem capable of valuing what we did win. They didn't seem able to appreciate the success on its own terms and they always wanted more. In one year we won the Intercontinental Cup, the Champions League and the European Super Cup: that's a fantastic set of trophies to win in a single year, but people started saying, "Madrid are going to win everything."

Now, hang on a minute, it's not that easy. And then what happens? Then we go two seasons, possibly three, without winning anything and the reaction is enormous, as if it was the end of the world

People say that Real Madrid were on the verge of creating history and then failed to complete the job, that it looked like we were going to mark an era, but didn't manage to do so. I disagree. I wouldn't say that the team was on the verge of making history. I would say that it *did* make history.

We won three Champions Leagues in five years: who else can say that? These days that is very, very difficult. No-one else has a record like that. Don't forget we also won league titles at that time. The only thing we didn't actually win was the Copa del Rey, the Spanish Cup. In Europe we were rolling over people, winning three Champions Leagues. Three in five years is historic. We did mark an era. We *did* make history for the club.

JAMIE CARRAGHER
DEFENDER 1997-PRESENT

BORN   28th January 1978, Liverpool
SIGNED   August 1994 as apprentice
LIVERPOOL CAREER*   400 games, 3 goals
HONOURS*   1 FA Cup, 2 League Cups, 1 Champions League,
1 UEFA Cup, 23 Caps for England
*Up to and including 1 March 2006

"We all dream of a team of Carraghers." That song echoed about Liverpool and, memorably, Turkey after Carragher's heroics in Istanbul in May 2005 wrote him indelibly onto the hearts of the club's fans. Rafa Benitez would probably concur that a team of Carraghers would guarantee a side with an impeccable will to win. Carragher has become recognised as one of Europe's finest defenders and his part in Liverpool's 2005 Champions League success left a string of quality strikers to vouch for his thirst for snuffing out their threat. Not bad for a boy from Bootle.

Liverpool 3 v AC Milan 3   *Liverpool win 3-2 on penalties*

Wednesday 25 May 2005

Atatürk Stadium, Istanbul
Attendance 69,000

Liverpool lift their fifth European Cup and win the right to keep the famous old trophy

Teams

Jerzy Dudek	Dida
Steve Finnan	Cafu
(sub. Dietmar Hamann)	
Djimi Traore	Paolo Maldini
Sami Hyypia	Jaap Stam
Jamie Carragher	Alessandro Nesta
John Arne Riise	Gennaro Gattuso
	(sub. Rui Costa)
Steven Gerrard	Clarence Seedorf
	(sub. Serginho)
Xabi Alonso	Andrea Pirlo
Luis Garcia	Kaka
Milan Baros	Andriy Shevchenko
(sub. Djibril Cissé)	
Harry Kewell	Hernan Crespo
(sub. Vladimir Smicer)	(sub. Jon Dahl Tomasson)

Gerrard 54, Smicer 56 Alonso 59	**Scorers**	Maldini 1, Crespo 39, 44

Referee: Gonzalez (Spain)

The room was quiet. Nothing was being said. Nothing could be said. We were 3-0 down in the biggest game of our lives. We were getting beat; make that getting slaughtered and, for now, what could any of us say? The only noise was the manager working away on the board trying to rectify the team and its tactics.

Suddenly, through the silence you could hear *You'll Never Walk Alone* as our fans incredibly found their voice once more. I'd like to say that it inspired me and made want to go out and claw the three goals back, made us turn in the performance of our lives to pull off that incredible comeback; but if I'm honest it just made me feel much worse. "They're doing their bit, but we haven't done ours," I thought. I was gutted. I felt like crying for them at that point.

They were singing away despite thinking that they were going to lose. I spoke to some after and the odd one was like, "I knew we were going to win," but I don't believe that for a minute. I certainly didn't think we could do it. But we did and what a night. What a crazy, unforgettable, amazing night.

It's got to go down in history as one of the best ever finals. People rightly go on about the 1960 game between Real Madrid and Eintracht Frankfurt and I think that the night in Istanbul will be the same. In twenty, no thirty years time people will still be talking about what was an incredible match. I have got about seven or eight years left of my career and I think if I am going to ever top that I'll have to play in a World Cup Final and score a hat-trick!

Watching us over the season you would never have thought that we could have created such excitement. Our league form had suffered badly as we progressed through Europe. Some of our players were better suited to the Champions League matches because, and this doesn't sound a nice thing to say about your own team-mates, it was less of a battle.

It's a totally different game in Europe, a different pace with different referees who look at things in a different way to our officials. We'd change our tactics in Europe, but that was down to circumstance more than anything. Fernando Morientes was cup-tied and Djibril Cissé had that hideous broken leg, so we had to play with Milan Baros alone up there and that made us stronger defensively.

Look at Luis Garcia. He was far more suited to Europe and he managed to score five or six very important goals for us. He was afforded more time and that suits Luis, who is still getting used to the rough and tumble of the Premiership.

Looking back you can cite the Olympiakos game as the night we started to approach the Champions League with real belief. Things like that win over the Greeks happen for a reason and the way we came back from two goals down to get the winner with four minutes left gave us such belief. I'm sure if you ask the guys who played against Saint-Etienne in 1977 they'd say that after that win they felt that this had to be their year. It was meant to be and that was the same for us after Olympiakos. You just felt that this was the prelude to something special.

But we hadn't seen anything yet. The Chelsea match was just one of the best. It was a privilege to not only be playing, but just to be in the ground. Usually when the game's being played it's hard to know what's going on in the stands, but we went out to warm up about half an hour before kick-off and all the old songs were being sung and you knew, you just knew that this was something different. I knew it was going to be a big occasion because our fans rise to those sort of games, but I also think that us scoring so early added to the passion.

Had Chelsea scored within five minutes it might have killed the crowd and then of course we had the six minutes of added time at the end where each person was on the edge of their seats. Scarves were being waved around everyone's heads and I remember thinking to myself this is like being in front of a South American set of fans. I've seen Boca Juniors on the television and that is what it is like. The energy was incredible.

I have played in a few great atmospheres, the night that Gérard Houllier came back from his illness against Roma in 2002 was one and, of course, being local boys, Stevie Gerrard and myself have grown up hearing about Inter Milan and Saint-Etienne. To hear that those who sampled those nights as players thought that they were matched by that Chelsea night is fantastic.

Not that it wasn't without its scares. Eidur Gudjohnsen had a real chance at the end. Jerzy went for a cross and missed it and then life became slow motion. Gudjohnsen shot and the fact that I never touched it into the net myself was unbelievable. I never knew where Drogba was and I just turned, thinking that the ball would be nestling in the net. Just thinking about it now sickens me, it really does. Imagine if we had got that close? There would have been no coming back then. I just lay there on the floor for about ten seconds and looked up at the sky feeling nothing but sheer relief.

The euphoria at the final whistle of that game basically continued until Paolo Maldini scored in the first minute of the final. The Chelsea win had brought such a sense of triumph to the city and to our fans who were convinced we were going to win the European Cup. As our run to the final had been so memorable, we travelled with all the fans' optimism.

I watch a lot of European football, though, and knew how good this team we were facing could be. A lot of our fans may have watched the second-leg against PSV and thought Milan might be a pushover. You only had to ask Manchester United's players and fans to know how special Milan could be. They had battered United, they really were brilliant. I knew we would find the final tough.

Try telling the fans that though. They were on a crest of a wave after the semi and who could blame them. What they had nicely chosen to ignore was how bad we'd been in the league. I went to Turkey thinking it was going to be a really tight game, but one we could nick. We'd done that against other teams on the way to Istanbul and if we could stay defensively strong, then we had the ability to score a goal to nick the game. I had a chat with Stevie the night before and we both agreed that it would be 1-0 either way. There wasn't going to be many goals.

A few of us had been involved in the UEFA Cup final in 2001 and we knew the key was to approach the game like any other. That, though, is easier said than done. In fact it's impossible. People are ringing and texting you non-stop wishing you luck, there's a mad clamour for tickets, and the buzz is almost unbearable.

We flew out two days before the match and the hotel was chocker with UEFA officials, ex-players, celebrities and press. It was as if the whole of Europe had descended on Istanbul for the match. It began to sink in just how big this was.

Rafa wanted to try and keep things as normal as possible, but he knew he was fighting a losing battle. The only thing different from the management's point of view was that we travelled two days before the game rather than the day before.

It was probably a good thing, getting us out of Liverpool. The atmosphere in the city was nuts with expectation. The local papers ran nothing but stories on the match, so it was quite a relief to leave and get away from all the hype.

I wasn't nervous, I'm not the type. I was more excited than anything. I'm about to play in a European Cup final and I just wanted to get started. I slept fine the night before, no problem. I had another kip in the afternoon. I never struggle sleeping. The game was on my mind though. Who would I be up against? How would the game go? You play the match in your head. I usually score the winner in those. In my head I wasn't worrying about them. I wanted to start the game well, get a few good touches early on; some good passes and relax into it. Ease in.

We couldn't have been better prepared. We had ten days between our last Premiership game and the final and so every day we were working on one thing, playing against AC Milan. We were recreating possible scenarios. How do we play if we are winning 1-0 with ten minutes to go, how do we play if we are 1-0 down with 10 minutes to go. Rafa's good, but even he didn't practice what we should do if we are 3-0 down at half-time!

We were all in the dark about the team the manager would pick, but I'd pretty much guessed a few days beforehand to be honest. I could work it out by the teams he was playing in training. Steve was being used in midfield a lot rather than off the strikers and so I realised that Harry might have a chance. Having said that, I thought Djibril Cissé would start, so I'm not as good a sleuth as I thought.

He didn't actually tell us the team until an hour and a half before kick-off. It was quite a shock to everyone because it wasn't how we'd played prior to the final, but as soon as it's named you have to get on with things.

The dressing-room was quiet, it always is before games. We don't have many shouters in the team and everyone looks after themselves. To be honest you're just making sure you're alright. Once the team is named I'm always first on the massage table. I usually hop up on that and relax with the programme. It's difficult, though, when it's in Turkish.

For the Champions League games you have to be there an hour and a half before kick-off, whereas it can be an hour back home. That leaves a lot of time on your hands, so we went out onto the pitch.

We knew how much money some of the fans had spent to get here and as we went out we thought, bloody hell there's more than the 30,000 everyone talked about here. The banners were all there. I loved them. Some of them even had my name on. God, that made me feel good. Every coach, every bus had something. I knew from my own family and mates how much the tickets were costing some. You were talking £1,000 and that's before you add the ale money.

The fans were a big part of the manager's final team-talk and he mentioned just how many had made the trip and that we had to do it for them. He talked about the contrast between the number of Milan fans and our own. It was three or four to one and that showed how much we mean to them.

Tactically, Rafa wanted to get at Milan, that was key. He'd studied videos and seen the damage that PSV had done to them in the semi-final and so that's how he hoped it would go. That's why he named that team. He was picking it to win.

We got out there and were all feeling well focused. I felt good and alert. We kicked off and then boom, we're losing. It was our kick-off! How did they score a goal from our bloody kick-off? Djimi Traore was a bit nervous and he lost the ball and then gave away a foul. From that free-kick they scored. We had built up for this for ten days, and then within a minute we were 1-0 down. You might as well be in the second-leg of a tie, and a goal down. None of us had had a kick and it's killed everything. The game plan, the atmosphere, it's all gone.

Mind you, for the next ten or fifteen minutes we played well and created chances. We were passing the ball well. John Arne Riise had a good shot, Sami had a good header, Luis had some half chances. It was going OK. We always wanted the ball, the full-backs were getting forward and we were going after the game. That, though, was to prove costly. As we went up the pitch, defending high, they could pick us off on the break. And, of course, they did.

Personally I felt good. After the goal, I had some good touches of the ball and was passing well. My whole mind was on trying to get us back into the game.

Soon though, Rafa had more to think about. Not only were we a goal down, but now Harry Kewell was clearly struggling and would have to come off. It was all going wrong out there. As Harry limped off there were some boos from the fans and that was tough. I can understand the fans' response. They weren't booing because he was limping off in a European Cup final. Anyone with a brain would know he was never going to fake that. I think it was a culmination of things. Fans hadn't been happy with him since he arrived, rightly or wrongly. He'd snapped his groin though. You had to feel for him. He's playing in a European Cup final, you do your groin and the next day you're having an operation. He wasn't feigning injury I can tell you. After we'd won he was singing and dancing like us all, but a few days later he was flat out. Having said that, I bet he'd rather have that medal than have played the whole game and we'd lost.

Replacing Harry was Vladi Smicer. It was a surprise to us that Vlad came on. I thought that Didi would be the replacement, but at only 1-0 Rafa wanted to keep his original shape. Vlad went onto the right and Luis played off Baros. It was to be an incredible night for Vlad, in what was his last game for the club. He was very worried before the game. For our last Premiership match against Aston Villa, he hadn't even made the sixteen. Luckily for the Champions League you get a few more substitutes on the bench and now he was in.

We were holding our own, but at times looked shaky. Djimi Traore was still a bit nervous and needed talking to. To be fair to him, to recover from the own goal he had scored against Burnley which knocked us out of the FA Cup back in January to win selection for a European final takes some doing. I needed to have the odd chat with him, though, because Milan were getting past him. We needed to hold a stronger line. He switched on and was immense in the second-half.

His confidence had been knocked by the goal and he was having to make split-second decisions against a player like Andriy Shevchenko. He was playing them onside by dropping deep too much, but, as I say, these are split-second decisions and Djimi had to make them. I shouted at him, but I was just saying that we had to defend together. He was defending as an individual and we had to become one rather than four.

We had our moments and Luis looked to have been fouled for what we thought was a penalty to us, but there was no time to dwell on it because the game hadn't stopped and suddenly you've got Kaka, Shevchenko and Hernan Crespo running at you. It was an amazing break. Kaka put Shevchenko in and he crossed it past me for Crespo to score. I was lying on the turf thinking, "2-0, that's it." At 1-0, I thought, "We're doing OK here, we might even get back in this," but 2-0 in a European Cup final, "This is going to be difficult."

Difficult was about to turn into nigh on impossible. Kaka played through a brilliant pass which I stretched for, but couldn't intercept. At the time I thought, "Oh shit, I've made a mistake there," but I've watched it back and realise it was just a class ball. I wasn't sure whether I could have stayed on my feet and got it, but it's such a great pass there was nothing I could do. Crespo's finish was incredible and, at 3-0, it's a rout.

Now I was just embarrassed. When you watch finals, no matter how big the gulf between the teams, they are always tight. You don't go 3-0 down before half-time in a European Cup final. It's not done. I was just gutted. I thought about my mates who had come as fans, spent a load of money and, when the whistle went for the end of the half, I couldn't get in the dressing-room quick enough.

If someone had said to me then, "This'll finish 3-0," I would have taken it. That sounds mad now that we won, but at the time I just wanted to stop the rot. I really was thinking that this could finish six.

We were devastated. A lot was made of Milan players singing victory songs at half-time, but I never heard any of that. Even if they were, you couldn't blame them, I think that's exactly what I would have been doing. They were about to win the European Cup. I think there was too much class in that Milan team, though, to start singing and dancing and I certainly didn't hear them.

The manager was calm. There was no big talk or anything. He just got on with sorting out the tactics and said, "Let's try and get the first goal." He was worried that Andrea Pirlo was controlling the game and by pushing Garcia and Gerrard forward they could stop him having so much of the ball. To be honest, I think he shared our worries that this could be five or six.

He was all set to bring Djimi off. He hadn't had the best of games, although he'd been better towards the end of the half. Djimi was all undressed and ready to get in the shower when Steve Finnan said his knee was sore and so Djimi's had to get dressed again, get his boots on and get ready to play another half.

We got out there, but again looked shaky and I remember Jerzy let an easy ball ricochet off his knees for a needless corner. I gave him a talking to for that one. I'll bollock anyone me. It doesn't bother me. The most important thing is the football match, it doesn't matter if you lose friends now and then, the most important thing is to win. Jerzy is fine though. He takes it all.

He made amends with a fantastic save from a Shevchenko free-kick and then Xabi Alonso had a good shot go just wide. The fans were lifted slightly, but it wasn't as if we'd piled on the pressure. After half-time if anyone was going to score it was going to be them again. It wasn't like we came out flying.

But then we did score.

Stevie's goal didn't have me celebrating. I calmly made my way back into position hoping that it had stopped the rot. That goal only gave us mild relief. At least we'd scored; it lessened the embarrassment. The fans started to sing a few songs and it got everyone out of the doldrums a little bit. Maybe in hindsight it just brought the Milan players down a bit.

They'd blown it the year before in the quarter-final against La Coruna after being 4-1 up from their home leg, and during this season PSV had come so close to beating them in the semi-final, so in their minds there must have been a niggling worry. If you look at their performance in the second half it would suggest that they lost it. We were good, but they were bad. For six or seven minutes they seemed so dazed. Their manager, Carlo Ancelotti, later called it, "Six minutes of madness." Milan weren't tackling us, we started to dominate possession and we went from there.

I was seeing a lot of the ball. We had three on two at the back so one of us could step out and being behind we had nothing to lose. I went for it and found myself getting up into their half. Now I could sense their fear.

When Vlad picked up the ball and banged it into the net our growing hunger for the task became real belief and their nerves became sheer dread. It was a great strike by Vlad, but the keeper might have a few doubts about himself there. It was a poor goal for them to concede. They gave it away and Vlad cracked a shot just inside the post. 3-2.

They shit themselves then. We were right back in it. I still didn't celebrate, I was urging us all on and from that moment each and every one of us wanted the ball, we were all so up for it and you couldn't help but feel that that we were going to get that third goal.

I surged forward again and played the ball into Milan Baros, who touched it in to Stevie. Milan didn't get the credit for that touch; it was great. He just nudged it round the corner and Steve's clear; flying towards goal. If that had been Bergkamp or someone like that they would have been raving, but Milan isn't known for that sort of play and it went unnoticed. I thought that was unfair.

You knew it was going to be a penalty because Steve's run was taking him across the defender and he's obviously going to be fouled. I still think Gattuso should have been sent off, mind. He was the last man. They said that Cafu was coming around to cover, but that was nonsense, he should have walked.

I followed up my forward momentum and ran into the penalty box. At the time I was sure that it was Nesta who had brought Steve down and I'm trying to get him sent off! I didn't realise it was Gattuso. I've got the wrong man. The Milan players were trying all the tricks and delaying the kick by arguing that it wasn't a penalty. I had the ball and Garcia came running over to take it off me, but I wasn't having it; "You're not taking it."

It had been agreed before the game that Xabi would be on them. He had never taken one in anger, but to be honest we didn't have a regular penalty taker. I gave the ball to him and then stood mid-way in the Milan half and watched. It all happened so quickly. Dida saved it low to his right, but you didn't have time to be gutted, Xabi's knocked in the rebound and we're back level. Unbelievable.

I've got the DVD and the fans are so funny. When we equalise everyone is going mad and there's this one fella who is just so shocked. He's just staring out into space in a daze. That always makes me laugh.

I didn't sprint over to Xabi; again I just got back into position. I was ecstatic, but I needed a breather because I realised this was about to get tougher. At 3-2 it was all adrenaline and you're hungry. At 3-3 I'm thinking, "We'd better watch ourselves here." That's when the fear arrived on our side of the fence. Now we've got back in it you dread throwing away all that hard work. Soon Milan emerged from their daze, got themselves sorted out and started to get their game together.

As time ticked on, Jerzy came for a cross and missed it and was lucky that Djimi was on hand to block a shot on the line. Again, I had to scream at Jerzy. We were so close and you don't want to lose to something stupid. If Kaka dribbles through five players and scores a brilliant goal then fair enough, but let's not lose this to a soft goal. We've worked too hard.

Ancelotti brought on Jon Dahl Tomasson for Crespo and I was well pleased. Tomasson likes to drop deeper and it meant life was a little easier for us. Crespo was very difficult to play against as he makes such intelligent runs and has a tremendous burst of speed over the first few yards and the best way to play him was to have the ball ourselves. Simple. That's what we did second half.

It was Xabi Alonso's form that allowed us to do that. His passing is as good as anyone in Europe. They had Pirlo doing the same in the first half, but Xabi in that second period was just as brilliant. His ability to keep the ball meant we had so much more possession and when we had it Milan couldn't hurt us. I was fortunate to have played in the reserves with Jan Molby when I was a lad. Xabi isn't quite at Jan's level yet as a passer of the ball, but he's not far off. He can use both feet and knocks it long and short to great effect.

It was adrenaline keeping us going. Milan had upped their game and we were tiring. Those incredible six minutes had taken it out of us, both physically, and, more importantly, emotionally. That kind of euphoria can be draining and we were hanging on with less than ten minutes to go. Fatigue was always going to come into this game and I found myself lunging in for tackles where I might have stayed on my feet. I was booked for a tackle on Shevchenko and got an evil glare from the Ukrainian as we jogged back. Oh well.

Ancelotti brought on Serginho. We moved Steve to right-back to cope with him because we felt Vlad might struggle. That change made us a little bit more defensive and I realised we could only hang on for extra-time and then penalties.

In injury time I played a poor cross-field pass that handed them possession. From that they broke into our box and had a man over. I had sprinted back thinking, "Please don't score from my cock-up," and found myself in the box facing their forward who was free out by the by-line. I knew the fella couldn't score from the angle he had and so there was no point me closing him down because he would have just pulled it back to Shevchenko. I read what he had to do and managed to block Shevchenko's shot and we won a goal-kick. That's my job. Block things, tackle. Strikers have to score goals and we defenders have to stop them. To me a last-ditch tackle or a clean sheet is like a goal.

It was tense. In the last minute Jaap Stam had a header that was going wide, but Kaka only had to touch it and it was in. He missed. It was so reminiscent of Gudjohnsen's miss in the semi-final. Things like that happen so quickly that you can't react, but if you look at Vlad's response on the line with his face in his hands you can see that our nerves were well frayed.

It was to be extra-time and, as knackered as we all were, we were just ecstatic about being in with a shout. Cissé had come on by then and Rafa just told us to play deep and compact. He hoped that the Milan defenders had tired and he wanted Cissé to try and hit them on the break. That was the plan, but I think he had one eye on penalties.

I was having treatment for cramp and focusing on the most important thirty minutes of my career, but as I lay there I was taken by the fans who were still giving it their all. They had played such a massive part in not only the final but over our entire run to get there. Olympiakos, Juventus, the Chelsea games. They had been incredible. The contrast alone between the two semis was unbelievable. Stamford Bridge was so quiet compared to Anfield and I know that all players say their fans are the best, but ours have proven it time and time again. I also know that they support a team who are successful so they get to sing at finals and in Europe, but look how they travel abroad with all the banners and all the songs.

The first-half of extra-time was very tight. Tomasson had one chance but Djimi did enough to put him off. The second period was all about us holding on. I stretched to stop a Serginho cross and my groin and my calves tightened with cramp. I was splayed out on the turf in pain. According to one TV pundit, who shall remain nameless, I had cramp in both groins! Our physio is being all nice and polite and waiting to be invited onto the pitch by the ref and I'm swearing. "Fucking get on, forget the fucking ref."

Rafa came over and thought I'd pulled my groin. We'd used all our subs, but I knew it was just cramp. I needed ten or twenty seconds without running and then went straight back on. The problem was, straight away another ball was whipped in and I've had to throw myself at it again. My legs were in bits.

There was no time to worry about that, though, as Sami and I were the busiest men there. In a way we relished it. As I say, it's your job and by the end we were both winning every header and getting first to every ball. Cramp or no cramp. It was the same against Juventus; out there in Turin we both were very comfortable despite the barrage they threw at us and in a perverse way you actually enjoy it.

In the last moments, though, Shevchenko had a header that we could do nothing about. He knocked it goalwards and from there it's slow motion again, you're just waiting for the net to bulge and to this day I can't believe he's missed it. Credit to Jerzy, he pulled off one amazing save and then followed up with another block, but it's a bad miss. I couldn't believe that once again we were still in the game and I just grabbed Jerzy and told him I loved him. I meant it too.

That was the end. It was penalties. The manager came to us all and asked who wanted to take one. I said I did and just thought I'd be having one. Then he read out the list and I wasn't on it. We didn't come up with a five beforehand because you don't know how people are going to feel afterwards. I thought Garcia would have one for example. He was always scoring them in training, but the manager thought he was too tired. In fact, all the subs took one, so the manager clearly felt it was best for the fresher legs to have them.

Before we got going I ran over to Jerzy and gave him a pep-talk. I don't care what you call it, cheating, gamesmanship, I just wanted to win the European Cup and I told him to do his best to put them off. Jerzy is a dead nice fella, probably too nice and I knew he'd be dead courteous to them and shake their hands. I said, "Don't worry about them. You don't know them, do you? Put them off lad."

It worked. Jerzy's giving it the Grobbelaar and they've missed their first two penalties and we've scored ours. When Cissé made it 2-0 you're starting to allow yourself to think, "We might win this." That was the first time I really did that.

Then it all changed again.

Tomasson made it 2-1 and John Arne Riise was up next for us. Riise's was a great pen, beautifully placed, but it was another great save. Dida blocked it. Because it's John, we all expected him to blast it, he's got a bit of a shot on him you know, but he's placed it and it hasn't gone in.

That let them back in and Kaka made it 2-2, so Vlad's penalty was vital. If he scored his, we really had a great chance. He knocked it in and went mad. He was celebrating like we'd won and I was telling him to come back and calm down. I didn't want him to get carried away because it can return to haunt you. All their players are watching him and I just thought this could get embarrassing. I remembered the Munich players getting a bit cocky in 1999 and then United came back to win, so you have to be careful.

They had to score their next penalty. I was standing next to Stevie and we see it's Shevchenko coming up to take it. There's no way he's missing, surely. Steve was up next for us, so I was saying to him, "Come on lad, you can win this for us." You don't expect the likes of Shevchenko to miss, but to be honest it was one of the worst penalties I've ever seen. It looks like he's trying to dink it, but it was nothing really. Jerzy got a good hand to it.

Pandemonium.

Suddenly my cramp's gone and I was off. I ran towards Jerzy, but then changed my mind and just wanted to be with the fans. Somehow I found my friends and family. I didn't have a clue where they were in the ground. My mates had come to the front. We did our celebrating and then, when I'd calmed down a bit, I went over and shook the Milan guys' hands. Stam came over and said, "Well done." They have to take some credit because they took it very well. I would have been suicidal.

To see that trophy with our red ribbons around it was emotional. I have always watched foreign football and I never thought I'd be playing in a Champions League final. Half-way through the season we were losing at Southampton, Crystal Palace, Birmingham, and Burnley even. You don't even entertain ideas that you could be involved in a night like this.

UEFA's President Lennart Johansson actually made to give me the trophy. He thought I was the skipper! Some of those old UEFA guys haven't got a clue, I don't think. Steve had probably been rehearsing that moment since he was a kid and can you imagine if I had lifted it? There would have been hell to pay.

We took the cup around to our fans and it was just singing and dancing. Johnny Cash's *Ring of Fire* had become our theme tune and all of us were banging it out. That song had started on one of the coaches that my dad had been on. They would bring music for the away games and that was on this tape. They started singing it and it's taken off. They play it at Anfield now. It's become our theme tune. All the players had a CD with it on and it's still funny to see the Spanish guys all humming away to Johnny Cash.

After all that celebrating the dressing-room was a bit of a come-down. You're that tired there isn't much more you can do. It sounds strange doesn't it, but we were so drained that back in the dressing-room, we just all sat looking each other. There were some big grins mind you.

Gérard Houllier came in and chatted to us. I gave him one of my shirts. That was nice. Liverpool is a real family and it was good to see our ex-boss. He must have thought of what might have been.

We had a room at the top of our hotel where we had a big party. I couldn't really enjoy it because my phone was going off every two minutes with people wanting to get in. I kept having to go down to the fella on the door and lie, saying that this was my brother and could he come in. "You have very big family," he remarked. I do, but it's not that big!

We had the Cup with us and there were speeches, but we were all tired. The game had finished at about a quarter to one local time, so by three we were all knackered. Someone said that Milan Baros had dented the Cup during the party, but I knew nothing about that. It's ours now, so it doesn't matter does it?

Coming home was amazing. The way we won the game brought them out in their droves. On rooftops, hanging out of windows, standing on cars.

Everybody you meet has a story about what they did or how they felt at half-time. None more so than Evertonians. In a local pub in West Derby all the Everton fans were doing a conga at half-time. A few lads I know wouldn't go out and watch it because if we had won they would have been sick. At half-time they all phone each other and say, "Let's get our gear on and go to the pub for a good gloat." They've got their Everton tops on and made their way out and as they walk into the boozer it's 3-3. How gutted must have they felt?

Another fella, this time a Red, watched the first half and went to bed because he's up early for work. A couple of hours later he gets woken up by fireworks going off on the street and he's thinking, "What is happening here?" He gets up and turns the TV on and there's Stevie Gerrard lifting the European Cup. Superb.

My medal sits proudly at home. My dad has been taking it around the local schools for the kids to have photos taken with it. I still have to double take when I see the words LIVERPOOL, EUROPEAN CHAMPIONS, but that's what that night made us and no-one can take that away.

I got married just weeks after the final and had the Cup at my wedding. We sat it on the top table. What a guest of honour.